WEB-BASED EDUCATION

WEB-BASED EDUCATION

Editor
Prof. Ramesh Chandra

Publications
KALPAZ PUBLICATIONS
DELHI-110052

WEB-BASED EDUCATION

Web-based Education

ISBN: 9788178351988

This book is Vol. No. 11 of Universal Education and Technology in 21st Century (Set)

Published in 2005 in India by
Kalpaz Publications,
C-30, Satyawati Nagar, Delhi-110052
E-mail : Kalpaz@hotmail.com

Laser Typesetting at : Master Computers, Delhi
Printed at : Ajit Printers, Delhi

Contents

Preface

The World Wide Web has introduced a new collection of educational opportunities for educators and students. The Internet is bringing us closer than we ever thought possible to make learning of all kinds, at all levels, any time, any place, any pace—a practical reality for every man, woman, and child. The web is a tool that empowers society to school the illiterate, bring job training to the unskilled, open a universe of wondrous images and knowledge to all students, and enrich the understanding of the lifelong learner.

The multiculturality of the Web explores how hyper-technology has supported, and can continue to support, several educational ideals consistent with multicultural education. These include inclusive education, collaborative education, and interactive education. If education is truly to be student-centered, then the experiences, perspectives, and ideas of the students themselves must be brought to the fore in the educational experience. To be 'included' in the educational process, students, as well as teachers, must be given opportunities to have their voices heard and to hear each others' voices. The Web is helping to facilitate this kind of inclusivity through countless sites that encourage teachers and students to participate in virtual global communities with other teachers and students who may be either very culturally similar or different.

But where there are new opportunities, they are usually accompanied by a series of new challenges. While training programs and instructional materials have made it easier for teachers to use the Internet more effectively in the classroom, recent research has shown that teachers still identify a lack of knowledge about the Internet as the primary reason they have not used it more often as a teaching tool. People who run Web servers usually do not screen Web site creators' credibility or qualifications on their site's content. This calls into question the accuracy and credibility of many Web sites.

When explored with a set of strategies that address these challenges, the World Wide Web has the potential to transcend the capabilities of many other multicultural media in its supplemental value to multicultural teaching practices. The key for unlocking this potential lies in understanding and using the Web not merely as an enormous compendium of informational resources, but more importantly as an interactive medium that can connect people across borders and boundaries. With this in mind, there are clear intersections between some of the important ideals in multicultural curriculum transformation and the educational opportunities presented by the Web.

Editor

Chapter 1
Multicultural Education and Technology

Multicultural education is a progressive approach for transforming education that holistically critiques and addresses current shortcomings, failings, and discriminatory practices in education. It is grounded in ideals of social justice, education equity, and a dedication to facilitating educational experiences in which all students reach their full potential as learners and as socially aware and active beings, locally, nationally, and globally.

Multicultural education acknowledges that schools are essential to laying the foundation for the transformation of society and the elimination of oppression and injustice. It relates to education and instruction designed for the cultures of several different races in an educational system. This approach to teaching and learning is based upon consensus building, respect, and fostering cultural pluralism within racial societies. Multicultural education acknowledges and incorporates positive racial idiosyncrasies into classroom atmospheres.

Since its earliest conceptualizations in the 1960s, multicultural education has been transformed, refocused, reconceptualized, and in a constant state of evolution both in theory and in practice. It is rare that any two classroom teachers or education scholars will have the same definition for multicultural education. As with any dialogue on education, individuals tend to mold concepts to fit their particular focus. Some discuss multicultural education as a shift in curriculum, perhaps as simple as adding new and diverse materials and perspectives to be more inclusive of traditionally underrepresented groups. Others talk about classroom climate issues or teaching styles that serve certain groups while presenting barriers for others. Still others focus on institutional and systemic issues such as tracking, standardized testing, or funding discrepancies. Some go farther still, insisting on education change as part of a larger societal transformation in which we more closely explore and criticize the oppressive foundations of society and how education serves to maintain the status quo — foundations such as white supremacy, capitalism, global socioeconomic situations, and exploitation.

Despite a multitude of differing conceptualizations of multicultural education, several shared ideals provide a basis for its understanding. While some focus on individual students or teachers, and others are much more "macro" in scope, these ideals are all, at their roots, about transformation:

— Every student must have an equal opportunity to achieve to her or his full potential.

— Every student must be prepared to competently participate in an increasingly intercultural society.

— Teachers must be prepared to effectively facilitate learning for every individual student, no matter how culturally similar or different from her- or himself.

— Schools must be active participants in ending oppression of all types, first by ending oppression within their own walls, then by producing socially and critically active and aware students.

— Education must become more fully student-centered and inclusive of the voices and experiences of the students.

— Educators, activists, and others must take a more active role in reexamining all educational practices and how they affect the learning of all students: testing methods, teaching approaches, evaluation and assessment, school psychology and counseling, educational materials and textbooks, etc.

The underlying goal of multicultural education is to affect social change. The pathway toward this goal incorporates three strands of transformation:

— the transformation of self;

— the transformation of schools and schooling; and

— the transformation of society.

Every child comes to school with an ethnic identity whether these identifications are conscious or unconscious. This identification must be recognized and respected by the teacher. It must be the basis for the learning activities in the classroom. The point here is to acknowledge differences rather than ignore them. It is equally critical that the children recognize and appreciate their own ethnicity and learn to appreciate those of the other children in the class. This recognition of individual ethnic identities is the beginning point, it is a connector of both the teacher to the student and the students to each other. It is the basic building block in the learning process which requires knowing where the child is relative to him/herself and the content to be addressed. This ethnic identification is a continual point of focus throughout the education process and is the basis for developing the next level of identification which is a national identification.

The national identity of the individual requires his/her understanding and commitment to the democratic ideals such as human dignity, justice and equality. Here the focus is on becoming effective members of a democratic society. An individual's strong national identification is essential to his/her development of a global identity.

As our society becomes more and more dependent on other societies, it is critical that the schools address the problems of the world as a whole. The development of the global identification provides the students with the opportunity to see how as a nation we fit into the world society. It allows students to better understand that the actions of a nation must not only be viewed in terms of the implications for that nation but what are the effects on the whole world. Children who have developed both a strong ethnic and national identity should have the perspective to also develop a global identification which should in turn make them better citizens of the world community.

At this point in time it is important to realize that the identifications discussed above are hierarchial. In other words the curriculum and the learning needs to proceed by first recognizing the ethnic identity, then the national and finally the global. The development of the latter are dependent upon the development of the former. It is also important that the individual identities are not static but continually evolving and so it is important for the curriculum to emphasize all three types of identities as learning progresses.

The metaphor of the melting pot is no longer functional. We have to switch to either the toss salad or the stew. It allows us to focus both on the differences in the ingredients while at the same time the beauty of the whole. a good salad does not have a bunch of components that look, taste or have the same texture. The success of the salad depends not only on its looks but also on a lot of other factors including the taste, the freshness of the ingredients, the smells, the textures and the mixture itself.

The goals of multicultural education are:

- To have every student achieve to his or her potential.
- To learn how to learn and to think critically.
- To encourage students to take an active role in their own education by bringing their stories and experiences into the learning scope.
- To address diverse learning styles.
- To appreciate the contributions of different groups who have contributed to our knowledge base.
- To develop positive attitudes about groups of people who are different from ourselves.
- To become good citizens of the school, the community, the country and the world community

— To learn how to evaluate knowledge from different perspectives.

— To develop an ethnic, national and global identity.

— To provide decision making skills and critical analysis skills so the students can make better choices in their everyday lives.

Multicultural education may increase the resentment encountered by students who feel that changes in school traditions, curriculum, and academic standards are not necessary to get along and respect students from ethnic minorities.

Since many institutions resist change of any kind, passive resistance on the part of the administration may simulate acceptance of the tenants of Multicultural education. Of course, excepting the tenants of multicultural education should be avoided with enthusiasm and optimism.

Multicultural education must have, as its crux, the below defining characteristics to achieve its purposes for students, teachers, parents, and administrators of the school system:

a) a learning environment that supports positive interracial contact;

b) a multicultural curriculum;

c) positive teacher expectations;

d) administrative support; and,

e) teacher training workshops.

If one of the features is absent, frustration and heightened resentment may occur as backlash behaviors multiply.

The effects of a positive multicultural climate may manifest in a number of ways, such as:

a) diminished pockets of segregation among students;

b) less racial tension in the schools;

c) increased ethnic minority retention and classroom performance; and,

d) inclusion of a multicultural curriculum.

The multicultural educational environment should not be a microcosm of our present society, with regard to issues of diversity and tolerance. Many factors determine a successful multicultural atmosphere, but the features as outlined above may be important indications of success.

Administrative support for multicultural education is critical. How can a house stand if the foundation is fragile. Multicultural education will be as successful as commitment to it by school administrators. Regardless of the level of commitment programs initiated under the guise of multiculturalism must receive reinforcement from administrators who are accountable for the success of established multicultural initiatives. A key factor in any proposed multicultural initiative is curriculum development.

A multicultural curriculum should be considered for several reasons:

a) provides alternative points of view relative to information already taught in most educational systems;

b) provides ethnic minorities with a sense of being inclusive in history, science etc.; and,

c) decreases stereotypes, prejudice, bigotry, and racism.

A significant demographic transformation is on the horizon for American schools. Educational institutions have been dictated too long by attitudes, values, beliefs, and value systems of one race and class of people. The future of our universe is demanding a positive change for all.

Multicultural Education and Technology

At its most fundamental level, multicultural education represents an orientation to schooling and the teaching-learning process that is grounded in the democratic ideals of justice and equality. Justice and equality have always been the focus of schools, but there is a substantial body of historical and contemporary evidence which demonstrates that the schooling experiences of most students of color, as well as many white students from economically poor and politically disempowered backgrounds, are inferior to those provided to white students from middle class, politically dominant backgrounds. Due to this disparity, proponents of multicultural education call for a studied restructuring of many of the long-standing policies and conventions of public schooling.

James A. Banks, professor of education and director of the Center for Multicultural Education at the University of Washington in Seattle, is recognized as a leading scholar in the field of multicultural education. He has detailed five critical dimensions of multicultural education:

1. content integration,
2. knowledge construction,

3. prejudice reduction,
4. equity pedagogy, and
5. empowering school culture and social structure.

Content integration: The goal of content integration is to expand the curriculum by incorporating contributions of diverse cultures into traditional disciplines of study. Arguably, this dimension is easily realized through technology. For instance, teachers at all levels have used the World Wide Web to extend the available learning resources. Electronic mail and multimedia technologies promote communication and interactions between diverse groups with the purpose of helping students learn more about content they study in subject areas as social studies, science, psychology, and even foreign language.

Many educators who acknowledge potential benefits of a merger between technology and multicultural education call for updating the physical infrastructures of schools. In schools where such updates (i.e., re-wiring) have occurred, teachers are making widespread use of the internet and other computer-based technology.

The knowledge and skills students acquire in these schools typically are being reinforced by computer availability and internet access in their homes. This reality contrasts sharply with that of students from poor/working class backgrounds who attend schools where the notion of re-wiring for internet access may seem superfluous in light of the absence of basic resources. Nor are these students likely to have internet access at home.

Citing a 1999 report of the National Telecommunications and Information Administration, Gorski reports that "African American and Latino households are only about one-third as likely to have access to the Internet from home as Asian, Asian American, and Pacific Islander households. The same group is only two-fifths as likely to have access as White households". This situation is reflective of the "digital divide" phenomenon. Thus, while technology can facilitate the content integration in the teaching-learning process, educators must be aware that in some circumstances this dimension of multicultural education will need to be addressed by other means due to lack of access to technology.

Knowledge construction: Knowledge construction dimension promotes critical literacy by examining the manners in which scholars and scientists contribute to their respective fields of study. Knowledge construction builds upon content integration by making explicit the worldviews and perspectives that inform knowledge claims. Similarly, it expands the legitimate sources of knowledge by helping learners recognize that their own experiences both within and beyond school are viable foundations for acquiring knowledge and skills.

Teacher educators are being called upon to use technology to promote and reinforce the knowledge construction process. Part of acquiring facility in knowledge construction is understanding phenomenon from the perspectives of others. To this end, teacher educators are making use of Internet technology to promote more critical engagement with subject matter. For example, Merryfield discusses advantages of threaded discussions in an online graduate course. Student-generated threads facilitate a class learning community that allows those of diverse cultural and national origins to perspective-take while simultaneously examining their own ideas about cultural diversity.

Prejudice reduction: Prejudice reduction is about eliminating all forms of bigotry. Also, it involves promoting healthy personal identity devoid of the tendency or need to denigrate those who differ from self. Multimedia presentations and distance learning technologies are being used to establish learning exchanges between students of diverse cultural backgrounds and thereby reduce prejudice and stereotyping.

Likewise, technology is being used to promote positive self-concept and foster positive relationships between students from diverse backgrounds in geographically diverse areas. Such efforts have included videoconferences, computer conferences, interactions on the Web, and e-pals. Technologies used with middle grade students have included interactive compressed video and use of two-way televised communication systems via telephone lines. Teacher education students are using distance learning technology, multimedia, and e-mail to engage in cross-cultural and diverse regional interactions with other prospective teachers.

Equity pedagogy: Equity pedagogy is about equalizing opportunities to learn. It involves incorporating various strategies and techniques that attend to learning styles and intelligence types. Writers interested in the nascent relationship between technology and multicultural education are discussing the urgency of using technology to address the various ways in which learners from diverse backgrounds best acquire school knowledge and skills.

Nevertheless, it is difficult to discern whether current efforts to merge technology and multicultural education are addressing this fourth dimension directly.

Indeed, some writers are concerned that technology may inadvertently privilege certain ways of processing information while it devalues others.

An important issue for many contemporary educators, particularly in the university setting, is whether internet technology is in any way superior to face-to-face instruction. It would appear that one advantage internet technology holds over face-to-face classroom format is in its ability to provide educators and students wide access to a cross-cultural professional and learning community. This can be accommodated through e-mail, bulletin boards, and chatroom sites.

Multicultural education proponents contend that in order to provide high quality experiences for all students, many traditional aspects of schools will need to be reconfigured. This is referred to as empowering school culture and social structures. Its ultimate purpose is to change the taken-for-granted policies and practices of schools that, while useful to some students, have greatly diminished the schooling experience for many others.

Online Technologies and Global Connectivity

Online technologies are one type of tool enabling global connectivity that can support constructivist classroom practices. With these technology tools, discourse communities are expanded to encompass interactions and collaborative exchange projects among peers from diversified cultural backgrounds. The expanded communities open opportunities for learners to interact with multiple perspectives that challenge their existing knowledge constructions and impose cognitive conflicts requiring negotiation. With the new online tools and their potential to enrich learning experiences beyond the capabilities of a traditional setting come new challenges for educators and educational researchers.

There seems to be a link between the technologies and authentic learning and collaborative learning in general; between technologies and student-centred, constructivist practices; and discussions in the literature examine those capabilities. However, educators are aware of the void in the literature of empirical reports testing the related hypotheses. Thus, there is an urgency to develop and implement research designs that accommodate the nuances of learning atypical of nontechnology, teacher-directed environments, as well as to explore alternative instructional paradigms that optimise the potential benefits of online technologies for learning. The internet is the world most powerful computer network connecting personal computers, sophisticated mainframes, and high speed supercomputers around the globe.

Because a myriad of computers and programmes are part of the internet, incompatibility problems can result because information is created using different computers and software. In 1989, a group of scientists at the European Laboratory for Particle Physics (CERN) in Geneva, Switzerland began developing an internet tool that would link information produced by all of the CERN researchers.

The tool provided a way to link textual information on different computers and created by different scientists. The object was to overcome issues of incompatibility and utilise a new way of linking made possible by computers, called "hypertext". Rather than presenting information in a linear or hierarchical fashion, hypertext permits information to be linked in a web-like structure. Nodes of information can be linked to other nodes of information in multiple ways. As a result, users can dynamically criss-cross the information web using pieces in the order most convenient to them. The CERN project resulted in an innovative front-end to the internet, now referred to as the World-Wide Web (WWW).

The WWW provides users with a uniform and convenient means of accessing the vast resources of the internet. In 1993, the National Centre for Supercomputing Applications (NCSA) at the University of Illinois pushed the CERN scientists' idea further by creating a software tool called Mosaic. Mosaic is an easy to use graphical user interface that permits text, graphics, sound and video to be hyperlinked. Mosaic was the first of the internet tools that are now referred to as "web browsers". Other well-known browsers include Netscape and Microsoft's internet explorer.

Web browsers permit users to connect to the internet and facilitate accessing information located on another remote computer. The web browser links to the remote computer just long enough so that the information you need can be sent to your computer for you to view.

Documents created to be viewed by a browser are formatted using Hypertext Markup Language (HTML). HTML solves incompatibility problems by using standardised tags which indicate such things as whether a piece of text should be plain, bold, italic, or linked to another piece of text. Pages of information on a computer formatted with HTML and accessible to someone with a web browser, are referred to as 'home pages' or 'web pages'.

The WWW have made the internet a more user-friendly environment. The ability to integrate graphics, text, and sound into a single tool means that novice users do not have to struggle with such a steep learning curve. In addition, organisations and individuals can create home pages independently and link to other home pages on their own computers or to pages created by others on different computer systems.

For educators, the WWW provides an exciting new opportunity for distance teaching and learning. The WWW can be used by the distance educator to build a classroom home page. The home page can cover information about the class including the syllabus, exercises, literature references, and instructor's biography. The instructor can also provide links to information on the WWW that would be useful to students in the class. Other links can access library catalogues or each student's individual home page. In addition, the home page can link students to a discussion list or listserv that set up for student communication. It is also a relatively simple matter to use the homepage to create forms that students can fill out and that will end up being sent to you as an e-mail message.

The WWW, allows more opportunites of interaction. The interaction itself is categorised within a learning context with the purpose of task/instructional completion or social relationship building, with a mixture of both types of interaction being common. Interactions should involve complex activity by learners to include engaging and reflecting, annotating, questioning, answering, pacing, elaborating, discussing, inquiring, problem-solving, linking, constructing, analysing, evaluating, and synthesising.

The levels of interactivity include:

i) interaction between participants and learning materials,

ii) interaction between participants and instructors/experts,

iii) interaction among participants, and

iv) management/feedback communications

Although content and social interaction are interwoven into highly interactive web-based courses, each will be discussed independently to further explain the role of both forms of interaction in a web-based course. Content interaction is based on the theory of learning that is most appropriate to achieve educational outcomes within the course itself. In many web-based courses, multiple layers of learning outcomes exist, thus suggesting that multiple strategies may be incorporated into the course. Some courses may include an intensive case study, while maintaining a weekly schedule of online lectures and discussion sessions. Other courses may adhere more loosely to a semester-long simulation with its outcome being an explanation of findings and events.

It is difficult to prescribe one best fit for content interaction, given the wide range of possibilities available on the World Wide Web. It is important, however, to ground the design of the learning environment in solid theory and pedagogy, as distance learning has been criticised for having very little, if any, theoretical context. Hannafin, Land, and Oliver discuss grounded design as a context for dealing with the range of design decisions that best facilitate learning outcomes. Grounded design is defined as the systematic implementation of processes and procedures that are rooted in established theory and research in human learning.

Social interaction is a key element in online learning. Given that the nature of online learning is anytime anywhere, the potential for isolation and frustration exist. The social interaction of the course must, at least initially, be designed into the course. Through collaboration and communication, the opportunity for learning more about peers and connecting with them in non-task specific conversation is more likely to occur. Although social interaction may have very little to do with a course, it is still valued as the primary vehicle for student communications in a web-based learning environment.

Non-task/content specific social interaction may include conversation in a chat room, inquiries about used textbook purchases, or questions about using a new version of a piece of software. When collaborative teams of students work toward project completion, there is still the need for relationship building in the learning community.

Relationship building is a necessary component of collaboration and communication and the perceptions of the efficacy of this type of social interaction can impact the learning outcomes of the course. By the very nature of social interaction, learners are directly able to foster content interaction.The overuse or misuse of interaction strategies can lead to boredom, overload, and frustration. It lessens the likelihood that students will be able to surmise what is important, and once again, frustration may occur when students perceive interaction as online busywork.

The more interactive the web-based course becomes, the more complex it is to use. For novice distance learners, complexity may very well lead to more frustration and isolation.

Future web-based tools hopefully will promote collaboration and interaction online in a much easier-to-use format. For now, designers of web-based courses should weigh the frequency and the quality of interactions required that best facilitate the learning outcomes to be achieved, where frequency does not always equal quality. The attributes of web-based instruction should be filtered through the philosophy and pedagogy that is presumed appropriate for the course, preferably adhering to the grounded design approach suggested by Hannafin. Oftentimes, lists of strategies and tactics are provided as design suggestions for web-based courses. When suggested out of context, it is difficult to surmise how the online experience may be structured. For example, in a list that suggests threaded discussions be used, there is still little detail as to how they are to be used within the learning experience itself. In a more behaviourist notion, threaded discussion may be used to elicit responses to given questions.

In a situated learning environment, threaded discussions may be used to discuss influences on the environment with a scientist in an attempt to determine why native plants are not surviving. Instructional content is the central component of a web-based course, as this is where new knowledge, skills, and abilities are presented. Whether students learn declarative knowledge or participate in a large-scale simulation, the way in which knowledge is shared sets the stage for all interactivity within the web-based course.

When given a choice, instructors many times will select land design instructional methods and techniques that are consistent with their theoretical and philosophical views. Instruction is presented either through an instructor-centred approach or through a more student-centred approach. There are times when one style of instruction is better than the other. When the outcomes of instruction are to analyse, synthesise, or evaluate, or when ill-defined authentic problems are the focus, a more student-centred approach would best facilitate the learning outcomes.

An instructor-centred approach would work well for instruction that is procedural, declarative, or well-defined in role and definition. Much of what exists online as web-based courses appears to have a strong instructor-centred influence. In much of the instruction, information is presented, examples are provided, practice exists, and in many cases, feedback is available through mentors and instructors. Student-centred learning is appropriate for outcomes of instruction that are focused on analysis, synthesis, and evaluation. Student-centred learning provides interactive, complementary activities that enable individuals to address unique learning interests and needs, study multiple levels of complexity, and deeper, understanding. Using open-ended strategies for learning, such as situated, learning, learners will actively construct meaning to determine how to proceed. This student-centred approach fosters a greater responsibility for learning and requires students to be more self-regulated in their approaches to learning. In some cases, scaffolding is provided that will facilitate self-regulation, thus providing strategies that students can use to create unique approaches to complex problems.Collaborative online learning environments is an obvious strategy for promoting interactivity. Many of the same factors that exist for campus-based students in collaborative groups parallel collaboration on the web. Topics such as group size, group role definition, group assignment and shared grading all are issues as well on the web.

A collaborative group's members should be committed to the "group goal" and to maximising each other's learning. Johnson and Johnson suggest very strongly that groups do not become collaborative just because someone assigns them together as a group. An effective collaborative group requires positive interdependence, group and individual accountability, promotive interaction, and interpersonal skill. Quality can be obtained through highly interactive courses. Occasionally, however, a strong collaboration component in the course may hinder some students' participation. If, for whatever reason, some students are unable to participate in collaborative, group building exercises, those students may be left to communicate with only the instructor or mentor. Many students complain about getting too much information online, not being able to follow concurrent threads in a threaded discussion, and not being about to keep up with multiple conversations occurring in chat sessions.

Despite some of the negative student comments, much can be said about conversation and e-discussion. Written communication seems to be more reflective, as students have more time to compose their thoughts and articulate in the manner intended online. Monitoring is essential for survival in a web-based environ-ment, even more so than in a traditional environment. This element of web-based design is not included, yet it is essential that work independently and can self regulate their own learning. Many cognitive strategies can be embedded within a web-based course, along with tips and ideas for time management and independent learning. Performance support can be defined as an electronic system that provides integrated access to information, advice, learning experiences, and tools to help someone perform a task with the minimum of support by other people. A review of the literature on EPSS suggests a series of goals and benefits of performance support, in prompting day-one performance. The basic premise of this just-in-time tool is to generate performance and learning at the moment of need, while assisting in building the knowledge infrastructure for work that will be done in the future. EPSS provides cognitive training wheels that can be progressively removed, as the performer no longer requires guidance and assistance.

Supporting performance for the technical and even motivational components of the course is important and must be considered when a web-based course is designed and presented. In addition to supporting entire programmes at a distance, performance support can also provide in course assistance.

Peer-to-peer interactive communication is another type of multi-way interaction between individual learners and the faculty member and commonly between learners and the learning group. This features is most often implemented with text chat; more sophisticated communication options are implemented with voice communications. May allow selective interaction between learners and/or instructor, but control of the conversation is shared equally among all participants. Web based delivery is attempting to address all three Learning Formats, with varying degrees of maturity and success. Successful distance education programmes seek to combine all three forms of learning in programmes of study.

Development of web-based courses can be very demanding, and often quite different from developing other kinds of media. Most self pace web based training includes the following features:

i) *Copiers*: Outline and overview to tell learners what the learning is about, what the learning goals are, how long it will take and what instructors expect of them.

ii) *Body content*: Must read area where you put your introduction and explanations, procedures and instructions. But remember, most users don't like to read a lot of copy on the screen so keep it short, simple and to the point

iii) *Demonstration or practice*: Demo, practice the lesson or simulate an environment, where possible.

iii) *A self checking quiz*: It gives trainees immediate answers and scores is part of the value added of WBT.

iv) *Help desk*. Provide an e-mail address or phone number on your WBT pages so learners know where to get help.

Online learning provides access to a potentially vast new student population. For students, the attractions are convenience and flexibility. Students can schedule schooling around their everyday lives without being constrained by the rigidity of regular class hours and the necessity of being in a physical classroom. Faculty members, on the other hand, are apt to feel concern and anxiety about engaging in this most-talked-about but never-experienced online teaching.

Integrating unfamiliar technology into one's instructional strategies can be stressful at first. Even good instructors who have experience using the internet for social and/or professional reasons can suffer from unexpected barriers to successful implementation, such as technology problems, student dropout, work overload, and overwhelming amounts of administrative housekeeping.

One of the top requirements for the success of distance education is the availability of quality faculty support. Post-secondary institutions commonly employ faculty development specialists to assist faculty members in their online course development. The number of these positions is growing at a fast pace.

Developing an online course is a complicated and time-consuming process, with many new and unique elements for instructors. Without the help of support services, developing and implementing successful online course can be an uphill battle. The demands that developing and teaching online courses pose to instructors are unique and novel. The faculty development specialists must accommodate the increased support needs of faculty. Instructors are likely to approach the project with a fair amount of anxiety, which is justifiable. In order to make the development process efficient and faculty-friendly, faculty development specialists must keep in mind the aspects of the course development process that facilitate success.

The goal of many online courses is the creation of a learning community, one where students and the instructor collaboratively share responsibility for the creation of joint knowledge as they jointly share responsibility in addressing learning tasks. Students who thrive in this environment tend to be more introverted in face-to-face situations, those who reflect deeply, are self-directed in their learning and are intrinsically motivated. Learners need to see the value of such learning properties engendered by this environment as collaboration, constructivism, interactivity, reflection, self-direction, individualisation, and experiential learning.

In the web-based course, a number of new communication elements confront the learner and must be addressed: asynchronicity, multiple conversations, interactivity, information overload, and pacing. Other online characteristics, such as social norms, instructor relationship, student role, and the academic atmosphere, are largely carried over from other school experiences. Students take these factors into consideration in developing learning approaches to work effectively online. Some are directly related to the technology, such as means of processing online information, deciding when and how to contribute, expressing oneself through written communication, dealing with multiple conversations and a deluge of messages, and determining interactivity.

Other learning strategies come from prior study patterns in school and work settings: setting goals, individualising assignments, managing time, establishing attitudes, and seeking and using feedback. To prepare students for learning online in their degree programme, Boise State University's (BSU's) Instructional and Performance Technology (IPT) programme offers an initial course that intentionally fosters student abilities to work with online distance technology while engendering study skills and explaining the importance of the required online participation. The syllabus explains the importance of participation—frequency, quantity, and quality of contribution—and the instructor works intentionally to maintain a strong online presence and respond with positive feedback. This has been a strong factor in lowering attrition rates in their courses. Several virtual degree-granting institutions have specific faculty development training for teaching effectively online, such as University of Phoenix's programme. Adult students who succeeded online were either technologically adept themselves; or had someone in their immediate support system who could readily assist them. Technical problems were found to be an obstacle for students taking web-based courses with the SLN.The most common practice is to have a help desk available to students for assistance with technical problems. Most programmes have a technician on call at all times by phone, fax, and pager, and then a technical support area online where support personnel can reply through e-mail or chat mode to more advanced questions.

Beyond just providing technical support, virtual institutions are using their help desks to route urgent administrative or academic requests to the appropriate office for timely attention. Redesigning a course for web-based delivery can be quite involved, requiring a steep learning curve, especially where there is limited institutional support for this activity. When a regular teacher decides to accommodate some distance students as well as the classroom ones, she or he finds there is twice as much work if taught like two different sections of the course.

Course developers and instructors are often part-time, adjunct faculty and may be doing this in addition to their other full-time jobs. To attend to all of the web conference areas can be demanding, especially when there are 15 to 25 students enrolled in a course.

Some educators claim that the time involved in delivering an online course can be up to three times as much as a face-to-face one, but this need not be the case it teachers and students budget their online time. Due to the emphasis placed on student participation, teachers need to shift roles to facilitating and managing peer-learning, instead of lecturing or inserting themselves as often into the discussion as they might in the classroom.

One approach for handling the increased workload is to provide a teaching assistant for each online course or have instructors co-teach the course with another faculty member. This allows for somewhat larger enrolments and improved instructional quality. There are institutions who have adopted an independent study model of web-based education that demands more investment in up-front course development, but can accommodate greater numbers of students without continual faculty involvement during delivery. For example, Brigham Young University's Independent Study programme allows students to start their courses on any date with a year to complete; they also provide automatic grading of web-based, multiple-choice assignments with immediate feedback. These courses are supplemented by related websites, multimedia resources on CD-ROM, and have optional online discussions with peers. The institutional dimensions of academic student support are similar to those faced by lower-tech delivery systems, but the college or university offering web-based courses needs to mount these services online. The provision of a web-based programme was a chief reason distance students chose the institution, and it is the means by which students interact in their courses. They expect that other communications with the campus about academic and administrative matters will be online as well. These fuller academic supports go beyond single-course interaction, and therefore require programmatic responses like:

— online counselling for educational adjustments and advising for degree planning;

— assessment for prior learning;

— student discussion areas;

— online career centres; and

— access to academic resources via the internet to support their degree programme study.

Students who lacked these environmental supports attributed their failure to external factors such as insufficient time, distractions, and circumstances that arose over which they had little control. Readiness is the major component of successful online learning. Readiness includes personal factors such as a compatible learning style, proficient computer skills, an interest in the content of the course, mastery of prerequisites, and good reading, writing, and keyboard skills. It also include, such environmental factors as having a quiet, roomy study area, a social network of family friends, and work associates that value the student's educational pursuits, a lifestyle with existence within it for distance study, and technical/institutional assistance in place for obstacles that might arise. Institutions are obliged to present realistic and accurate information about course demands, but their marketing efforts sometimes overshadow this voice. Effective counselling as the primary means of accomplishing this. This role, assumed by full-time counsellors, tutors and support staff means being supportive, encouraging, and pastoral to some extent. Such counselling sets forth realistic expectations about online study demands for working adult students who have been away from college and/or never juggled their education with other roles they must play. The counsellor suggests, needs to let students know that it is those who take direct responsibility and control of their college experience that prove to be most successful. This counselling can also address the readiness factors listed above and assist students with time management, organising their situation for a successful educational role and activities, and garnishing support from spouse, children, and their employer.

Online learningcourses generally have an important advantage over independent study, because the online class has a fixed schedule with a dedicated professor assigned to the course. Rapport develops through supportive online interactions, and an astute online faculty member will pay attention to students who seem to be falling behind in their web-courses and give them private notices of encouragement and support, i.e., assuming the counselling role. Suny Empire State College's Centre for Distance Learning provides an example of such counselling support. Once admitted, each student is assigned an advisor who mentors them throughout their individualised degree programme. With that advisor, they take a required independent study in their first enrolment that addresses many of the readiness issues outlined above, as well as allows them to assess their academic abilities and career aims. For many years distance programmes have accepted most standard forms of prior learning credit as it related to the student's degree programme, such as accredited college transcripts, CLEP test scores, and ACE, PONSI, and DANTES recommended credit equivalents. However, individualised credit by evaluation (CBE) was restricted to in-person settings. No longer will this be the case, however. SUNY-ESC's Centre for Distance Learning has begun individualised CBE in common areas, done at a distance through e-mail, the phone, and mail and such an web-based environment is being designed. Other virtual supports are social in nature, such as announcement areas, student bulletin boards, and topical conversation areas; these integrate students with their peers, create an online Community of scholars, and create institutional affiliation.

The British Open University (BOU) Students' Association maintains several hundred such conferences covering the gamut of topics to bring together its student body. It operates a bulletin board for events and activities of student interest. A majority of adult distance students pursue further education for career advancement or change. These individuals are returning to college as necessity learners—where education is essential for them to keep or obtain a job—or as rainy day planners—where education provides a safety net to give them options if opportunities come up or something goes awry in their current position. Therefore, an important student service on the virtual college site would be a career centre. Such a centre could have such features as information about jobs and employment; career testing and counselling; networking about jobs with other students, university personnel, and alumni; as well as links to online job search services. The library is a key component, of quality education, and academic institutions have a responsibility to provide external students with resources, facilities and services equivalent to their internal peers. The virtual institution must provide an online bookstore for students to order course guides, textbooks, and major instructional resources for their online course. Other resources could include lab kits, calculators, CD-ROMs, computer software, audio and videocassettes, and so forth. Such facilities will allow students to purchase materials by courses as separate components, paying for their purchases online by credit card. Increasingly these institutions will compete with local bookstores, conventional bookstores that sell textbooks online like Barnes and Noble, or online bookstores like Amazon.

Distance students are expected to use libraries like their campus counterparts; fortunately many of these services are going online as well. Reference librarians are available on the web or by toll-free call to answer specific research questions, as are online interlibrary loan services. Distance libraries allow online students to search databases that may only have citations and abstracts, and then allow them to retrieve the documents from their own collections for modest photocopying and mailing fees. For book check-outs, these institutions have an online circulation desk that allows for longer periods to compensate for postal mail exchanges. Libraries employ user identification and password procedures to ensure that only genuine students of the institution can use online subscription services for which it pays fees. The WGU has established an electronic reserve, putting an electronic version of an article or a chapter of a book on a password-protected website for a limited period of time.

Often, distance students can, purchase access to a local academic library in their community or region for a nominal fee and use interlibrary loan services at their local library for books. High quality academic resources are being made available through the World Wide Web, but sometimes it is difficult for distance students to judge the academic quality of these sites. Institutions like the University of California at Riverside, have created an online service, Infomine that recommends 15,000 university level web links by academic area. The WWW Virtual Library provides a similar service.

Distance educators should integrate information gathering and evaluation skills into the distance curricula as it has on campus. Additionally, libraries must get students familiar with their services and raise their expectations to use what online information resources are currently available. In concentrating on the individual course interactions, institutions have often neglected the fuller academic resource supports necessary to mount full-service web-based degree programmes.

Although distance educators think it would be a good idea to create greater institutional affiliation by bringing together distance students online and provide the services outlined in this section, few have fully developed these web-based environments to make these interchanges possible. One of these difficulties is reliable dial-up Internet service when the campus acts as an Internet Service Provider (ISP). For on-campus students this internet connection may be supplemental to on-campus services; to the distance student it is a continuous, absolute necessity for academic and administrative support. Some supports are strictly operational, providing students with efficient institutional services through web-based communication and information technologies.

CHAPTER 2

Web-based Multicultural Education

The internet is bringing us closer than we ever thought possible to make learning of all kinds, at all levels, any time, any place, any pace—a practical reality for every man, woman, and child. The web is a tool that empowers society to school the illiterate, bring job training to the unskilled, open a universe of wondrous images and knowledge to all students, and enrich the understanding of the lifelong learner. The opportunity is at hand. The power and the promise are here.

The multiculturality of the World Wide Web explores how hyper-technology has supported, and can continue to support, several educational ideals consistent with multicultural education. These include inclusive education, collaborative education, and interactive education.

Online is a collection of strategies for using the Internet to expand your resource base across physical and cultural boundaries and participating in a border-crossing dialogue on multicultural and education-related issues. Resource listings and instructional pieces will help you find and use web sites and forums designed for this purpose including discussion boards, listservs, and chat rooms.

The World Wide Web has introduced a new collection of educational opportunities for educators and students. But where there are new opportunities, they are usually accompanied by a series of new challenges. While training programs and instructional materials have made it easier for teachers to use the Internet more effectively in the classroom, recent research has shown that teachers still identify a lack of knowledge about the Internet as the primary reason they have not used it more often as a teaching tool. More challenges arise when teachers do become cyber-savvy. For example, information on the Web is not static.

People who run Web servers usually do not screen Web site creators' credibility or qualifications on their site's content. This calls into question the accuracy and credibility of many Web sites. When explored with a set of strategies that address these challenges, the World Wide Web has the potential to transcend the capabilities of many other multicultural media in its supplemental value to multicultural teaching practices.

The key for unlocking this potential lies in understanding and using the Web not merely as an enormous compendium of informational resources, but more importantly as an interactive medium that can connect people across borders and boundaries. With this in mind, there are clear intersections between some of the important ideals in multicultural curriculum transformation and the educational opportunities presented by the Web.

Interactive Teaching and Learning

A vast network of teachers and students around the world and across myriad cultures who have read a particular textbook, gathering somewhere to share questions and exchange resources on a given topic.

The interactive opportunities can transcend the potential of most other educational media as a means to connect students with first person sources beyond classroom walls and national borders and across cultures. Most Web site creators provide an email address and/or other contact information so that teachers, students, and others can, in fact, contact them with questions, challenges, critiques, or comments.

Many educators understand Inclusive teaching as incorporating diverse voices and perspectives in the classroom. To them, inclusion is about finding materials and tools that are representative of the students in the classroom. Multicultural education takes this concept a step further.

If education is truly to be student-centered, then the experiences, perspectives, and ideas of the students themselves must be brought to the fore in the educational experience. To be "included" in the educational process, students, as well as teachers, must be given opportunities to have their voices heard and to hear each others' voices.

The Web is helping to facilitate this kind of inclusivity through countless sites that encourage teachers and students to participate in virtual global communities with other teachers and students who may be either very culturally similar or different.

Collaborative Teaching and Learning

Collaborative and interdisciplinary teaching and learning are concepts that have been introduced, attempted, and reintroduced for decades. It is not uncommon for a group of teachers from a particular school to combine efforts in an attempt to connect lessons from subject to subject. In fact, for many teachers who struggle with time constraints and burn-out, sharing resources and collaborative planning become vital aspects of day-to-day classroom operations. For others, it is an avenue for modeling constructive and cooperative bridge-building across groups. As with Interactive and Inclusive teaching and learning, the Web has the potential to greatly expand the breadth and depth of collaborative possibilities of educators.

Despite the wonderful multicultural and educational potential the Internet holds, the very feature of the Internet that can facilitate Interactive, Collaborative, and Inclusive teaching and learning - interactivity - remains sadly untapped by educators. Like no previous medium, the Internet can facilitate cross-cultural communication, interpersonal bridge-building, and intercultural networking. It can expand your resource base virtually infinitely and diversify it to a previously unthinkable extent. Below are some strategies for using the Internet to do just that - expand your resource base by networking across cultures, national boundaries, and even comfort zones.

Several email discussion forums (also known as listservs or mailing lists) exist that deal specifically with multicultural education and related issues. Participants can post messages (questions, comments, responses, etc.)

to a list address, and those messages are then circulated to the rest of the forum's subscribers via email. Like discussion boards, email forums provide participants with the opportunity to network with other people interested in a particular topic and to engage in challenging and thought-provoking dialogue on a variety of issues.

Email forums tend to be more intimate and personal than discussion boards. Because people generally participate in email forums over a considerable length of time, the names and email addresses flashing into everyone's mailbox can become familiar. This can provide an opportunity to make more personal connections with other educators or activists from around the world.

Several recent studies indicate that the primary reason teachers give for not incorporating computer technology into classroom practice is a lack of training or knowledge about how to use products such as CD-ROMs and Web sites. Educators, already pressured by time constraints, are often intimidated by a perceived learning curve when it comes to developing better computer skills.

For many, this feeling is exacerbated when they finally learn enough about the Web to navigate around cyberspace and do simple searches, and suddenly find themselves lost in a maze of broken links, pornographic sites, and educational sites that have little or no original content or that have not been updated since 1996.

Several media and educational organizations are familiar for producing TV shows, films, CD-ROMs, books, and other teaching and learning materials that support multicultural ideals and curriculum development. The National Geographic Society, the

Discovery Channel, the Public Broadcasting Company (PBS) and others have been part of many of our classrooms for years.

Like other educational organizations and companies, National Geographic, PBS, and others recognize that in order to remain competitive in today's market, they need to include a strong and visible Web presence among their multiple projects. As a result, they have developed a series of techniques and strategies for attracting Web users to their sites. One strategy many organizations employ to bring users to their sites is to provide free educational materials and resources. In fact, there seems to be a competition brewing among those companies known for producing educational media to offer more, and better, resources than their competitors. Teachers and students are among the winners of this competition, reaping the benefits of several sites scrambling to outdo their competitors.

Companies that are already known for producing quality educational materials have a vested interest in offering only well-researched and well-evaluated resources. So one simple strategy for digging through the dirt to find quality classroom resources on the Web quickly is to turn directly to the Web sites of National Geographic Society, the Discovery Channel, and others who have a reputation for producing effective educational media and whose products have been proven effective in your classroom.

In many cases, these sites offer entire sections such as "Teaching Tools" or "Lesson Plans" or "Student Resources." Many actually host online learning activities for students and discussion forums for educators. Some allow you to download a variety of educational materials including maps, audio and video clips, worksheets, and historical documents. And again, companies who have built reputations by producing and supporting quality educational projects and resources know that it is in their best interest to provide only high quality resources through the Web.

There seem to be hundreds of "Multicultural Education Links" pages or general multicultural education pages that are comprised entirely of links to other sites. What makes these sites confusing and frustrating is that they are often linked to each other. A user can spend hours linking from one list of links to another, and so on, without ever finding original resources, teaching tools, or interactive opportunities.

Most of the criteria used to assess and evaluate traditional educational media such as textbooks and films can be directly applied to Web sites as well. These include: accuracy of the information, critical analysis of possible bias, credibility of the author and/or publishing source, appropriateness and accessibility to the specified audience, timeliness, relevance to a particular subject area, validity of content, and effectiveness of aesthetic aspects. Still, for a variety reasons, even deeper considerations for some of the more traditional educational evaluation criteria and several new criteria must be added to old models to holistically evaluate products of this fairly new cyber-medium.

For instance, unlike traditional educational media such as films, textbooks, and journals that usually go through a rigorous review process before being made widely available to teachers and students, virtually anybody with access to a Web server can create an educational Web site.

In most cases, there is no entity comparable to a publishing company to help ensure the credibility or expertise of educational Web designers. Likewise, as is the case with many journals, there is no formal review board to examine the validity of the information on most educational Web sites. For the most part, the responsibility is left with the user to assess these issues.

Other complications to the assessment of Web sites exist within the structure of the medium itself. In no other medium is the line between commercial and informational distinctions quite so blurry. Sometimes it is difficult to ascertain whether a particular site is a purely commercial venture or a purely educational venture. In fact, it might well be the case that no site fits the latter extreme. Again, since many Web sites are produced by unfamiliar sources, we, the users, must look deeper to uncover the bias of an educational Web site.

In addition, unlike in books or films, the information on Web sites is not static. This can be a strength, allowing site maintainers and authors to continually update material. Literally hundreds of models for evaluating Web sites have been created by university librarians, educational and instructional technologists, and Web developers. Some of these focus on content credibility and validity while others focus on design and navigability. There is sometimes a tendency in education to use new technology for the sake of using new technology and without a particular need or sense for how it will improve curricula or pedagogy. As somewhat of a cautionary measure, this category may appear to be an obvious first step in assessing a Web site or any educational product. It explores the extent to which the content and target audience of a site match with your needs and target audience.

One cannot assume credibility or expertise in regards to a Web site as readily as they might with a textbook. We must be conscious of credibility both in terms of the author's authority and the trustworthiness of a site's content. Again, this is a step that should be taken in relation to all educational media. It is not always so much about what information is included - we must remember to also ask what is NOT included. These criteria critically examine the inclusiveness of a site or whether the author is up-front about its exclusiveness.

The foundation of a multicultural curriculum is accuracy and completeness. This category addresses both of these intertwined concepts.The internet was originally designed to give people access to each other and information. If a resource is inaccessible because of coding problems or incompatibility with certain browsers or special-needs users, it fails to meet even the minimum requirements for an effective educational tool. And if a site author or sponsor is inaccessible through the site, she or he fails to take advantage of the fundamental nature and value of internet technology. This criteria category covers accessibility of the site as well as accessibility of a site's author or sponsor.

The Web has the capability to house educational opportunities consistent with the principles of multicultural teaching and learning to a greater extent than any other medium. Amidst all of the hype about the Internet is the reality of its inevitability. Forged by the competitive struggles of the private sector, it will soon surpass today's expectations like a Ferrari overtaking the Model-T. Web-based education is just beginning, with something of far greater promise emerging in the middle distance.

Yet technology, even in its current stage of development, can already allow us to realistically dream of achieving age-old goals in education:

— To center learning around the student instead of the classroom

— To focus on the strengths and needs of individual learners

— To make lifelong learning a reality.

Development of Web-based Education in USA

The US Web-based Education Commission set out to discover how the Internet is being used to enhance learning opportunity, and to identify ways that Congress and the President can help local schools, state education agencies, and postsecondary institutions overcome barriers. Its work began with face-to-face hearings across America and in virtual hearings on the Web. The Commission listened to hundreds of people eager to show how the Internet and learning are coming together to meet the needs of their communities and schools. The commission found that, the baby boom echo, the 25% increase in the US birthrate that began in the mid-1970s and peaked in 1990, and rising immigration have increased school enrolment. Public elementary and secondary school enrolment is projected to reach over 47 million in 2000, and to increase further in subsequent years. Schools across the US will need to hire between 1.7 and 2.7 million additional teachers over the next decade to meet the demand of rising enrollments and replace a large pool of retiring teachers. $127 billion in spending is needed to repair, renovate, and modernize school buildings. The average public school in America is 42 years old.

The Commission listened to those who are concerned about preserving the most valuable elements of traditional education delivery as we move ahead in developing web-based courses and models. They told to the commission the Internet offers education in places where there is none and extends resources where few exist. They told the commission that the Internet connects people, communities, and resources to support learning. They told that it extends the learning day and the learning place. They showed how it adds graphics, sound, video, and interaction to give teachers and learners multiple paths for understanding.

The Commission listened to people facing problems as varied as all of America. The solutions they created were no less diverse. Every person who testified before the commission had one thing in common: each was an Internet trailblazer who heard the cries of need in their communities, and responded-crafting solutions that best fit local outlooks and expectations. Each saw an opportunity and took it. Each accepted risk. Each embraced a challenge.

It is an empirical success in schools, and an empirical success in the private sector. Imagine what would have happened if the US's corporate leaders had imposed a similar moratorium in 1990, before they were able to measure objectively any positive impact of technology investment in productivity. It took years for these technological investments to bear fruit. Fortunately, business made these investments in technology.

It is the beginning of a new way of learning. In one sense, however, those who urge education to hold back have nothing to worry about. A de facto moratorium already exists in most American schools. On average,

U.S. firms spend between $3,500 and $5,500 per worker in technology and technological support each year, compared to per student spending on technology that rarely exceeds a couple hundred dollars in the best of circumstances.

At the beginning of the 21st Century, the most cutting edge tool to be found in many American classrooms-including institutions of higher education-is still an overhead projector.

Today's education is built on an agrarian model that worked in the years. Schooling changed to take on elements of the industrial revolution (factory-line classes, assembly-line curriculum, and teacher-foremen) that worked for the needs of the Industrial Age. New designs are needed to create the "knowledge workers" who will define the Information Age. The market is there. Business is poised to support education with powerful Internet solutions.

Education itself can be a strong market that drives the innovation of continuing products, tools, and applications to benefit learners across the spectrum. The global economy is there. If this era of globalization has proven anything, it is that a growing world economy can create a strong and lasting demand for skilled knowledge workers and a technologically savvy workforce. But we haven't made the connection to education. We must seize the opportunities and complete these connections-technological and human. And we must advance with constant assessment and reflection. There is still much about learning and the impact of technology we do not know. We must continue to research what is not known, analyze what is proposed or underway, and then examine the results.

To make the most of learning with the Internet, we will have to address serious issues. Many of these issues are not new. They have been facing education for decades, and some are reaching a crisis point.

The Internet is not a panacea for every problem in education. We need to be realistic. But we also must realize that the Internet is a tool that can help us empower every student and elevate each individual to new levels of intellectual capacity and skill. That is the great opportunity of this new technology. Such a promise is easily made. It will take a greater commitment to keep. Moving to:

— broadband

— multimodal rich connectivity

— untethered (wireless) access

— the technology adapting to the user

Moving from:

— narrowband

— plain, single mode (e.g., text or speech)

— tethered (wired) access

— users adapting to the technology.

Technology trends

Education and training is the second largest sector of the U.S. economy. At approximately $815 billion, it represents the US's second largest expenditure, behind healthcare. The education market currently represents approximately 9% of the gross domestic product. The K-

12 e-learning market is estimated at $1.3 billion and is expected to grow to $6.9 billion in 2003. The Internet offers one of the most promising opportunities in education ever. And yet they were troubled by their inability to harness its potential advantages.

E-learning Opportunities

The US Web-based Education Commission heard from hundreds of trailblazing heroes around the teachers, principals, and superintendents; local and appointed officials at all levels of government; higher education faculty and administrators; content developers and telecommunications providers; researchers, parents, and students. They shared powerful visions. Their online participation itself was an eloquent demonstration of the power of the Internet. They urged the commission to seize the opportunity. They showed a need for changes in policies and priorities that can only become more acute as this technology matures. From their testimony, the Commission heard a need for:

— Broadband Access

— Professional Development

— Research and Development

— Quality of Content

— Regulations and e-Learning

— Privacy and Protection

— Funding

— Powerful new Internet resources, especially broadband access, that is widely and equitably available and affordable for all learners

— Continuous, relevant training and support for educators and administrators at all levels

— New research on how people learn in the Internet age High quality online educational content that is widely available and meets the highest standards of educational excellence

— Relief from outdated regulations that impede instructional innovation in favour of approaches that embrace anytime, anywhere, any pace learning

— Safeguards to protect online learners and ensure their privacy, especially that of young children

— Sustained funding-via traditional and new sources-that is adequate to the challenges at hand.

The Commission's recommendations rest on the conviction that solutions come not from the top down, but from all levels of stakeholders in America's educational and economic future. As such, the commission is issuing a call to action that is addressed to policymakers and politicians, college presidents and parents, teachers and teacher educators, and students and business leaders.

Broadband Access

For students to learn with the tools and content of the Internet, they must have ready access to its supporting technology. But even the term access must be more sharply defined. "Access" is more than getting one's hands on a computer, or simply connecting to the Internet. Access must be convenient and affordable. It must offer a user the opportunity to find and download complex, content-rich resources. The technology that supports access must be where the learner is located and be available whenever he or she needs it. Access may take place in the school or college or adult literacy classroom, in the library or after school center, in the community center or workplace, or in the home.

Those who work with the technology that supports access must have the skill and understanding to apply it well. If the user-whether teacher or learner, parent or administrator-does not know how to work with technology or where to go on the Internet to find material of value, that learner does not have real access to what the Internet offers.

Access also implies that once a user has the connection and is able to use it, he or she can find content and applications that have meaning and value for his or her learning needs. Much of the content on the Web is created for adults, not schoolchildren. And little is written at a level that works for the 44 million Americans who read below the average literacy level. Non-English speakers and those from other cultures find little on the "shelves" of the Internet that speaks to them or to their interests.

Without broad access, there will be little demand for the innovative content and applications that can bring new teaching techniques and new assessment models. Without access, teachers cannot benefit from the just-in-time training and support the Internet has made possible in other professions. Without access, schools and universities will not have the links that could move research into practice and practice into research.

In its purest sense, broadband refers to the transmission of large amounts of data electronically, whether through wire or wirelessly. The more powerful the capability to transmit data, the richer the online experience. For education, broadband access means the elimination of time and distance from the learning equation.

Broadband carries with it powerful multimedia learning opportunities, the full interactivity of instructional content, and the quality and speed of communications. Broadband access today is 50 to several hundred times more powerful than its precursors. Broadband access tomorrow holds even greater promise.

The promise of widely available, high quality web-based education is made possible by technological and communications trends that could lead to important educational applications over the next two to three years.

The first trend is toward greater broadband access and better data packet handling capabilities resulting from the new "Internet2" project. For learners this will mean a richer delivery of content than today's delivery of simple text. Tomorrow, higher "bandwidth" will enable richer interactive environments.

The second trend is that of pervasive computing, in which computting connectivity, and communications technologies connect small, multipurpose devices, linking them by wireless technologies. It is much cheaper to build cellular relay stations than lay miles of cable. Wireless solutions may enable underdeveloped and remote areas to quickly take advantage of the Web via wireless phones, two-way pagers, and hand-held devices.

Over 30 years ago, large-scale testing, deployment, and development by the academic community leveraged sustained federal investment in fundamental technologies and set the stage for the Internet's commercial success. Applications such as e-mail and the World Wide Web, initially developed to enable collaboration among researchers, have transformed the way we work and learn.

Today, academia, government, and industry are once again working together to sustain the same partnership that nurtured the Internet in its infancy. This partnership is developing, testing, and deploying the high-performance Internet technologies required to enable a new generation of network applications.

"Internet2" and the Next Generation Internet (NGI) initiatives are among the efforts in this area. Internet2 is a consortium led by over 180 U.S. universities working with over 70 leading companies to develop and deploy advanced network applications and technologies for research and higher education. Internet2 members work closely with agencies participating in the NGI. Of major significance for K-12 education, states and districts with existing networks will be able to apply to the NGI to participate in the vast opportunities provided by Internet2 access.

High-performance networking enables applications that can provide qualitative leaps beyond what is possible using today's Internet technology-

— *Digital libraries*: HDTV-quality video and CD-quality audio available on-demand will enable students to search interactively, and access and retrieve information previously available at only a few locations.

— *High-fidelity collaboration*: "tele-immersion" and other technologies will allow teachers and students separated by hundreds of miles to interact with each other as if they were sitting across the table.

— *Virtual laboratories*: remote access to scientific instruments will extend to the classroom resources such as mountain-top telescopes and electron microscopes.

Applications enabled by high performance networking hold the promise to transform education. Just as the Web was unanticipated only a decade ago, tomorrow's Internet may provide us with capabilities and possibilities we have yet to imagine.

The third trend is digital convergence: merging the capabilities of telephone, radio, television, and other interactive devices. The ubiquitous infrastructure of television will be significantly enhanced by conversion to digital transmission, which has been mandated by the US Federal Communications Commission (FCC).

Through this increased capability, stations can offer dramatically enhanced programming by "datacasting" a wealth of supplemental information to accompany the regular broadcast. This may include course materials, software, and reference guides delivered via text, video, or audio formats. Direct satellite connections to the home offer another pathway for rich content.

The fourth trend accelerating the pace of educational technology advances is the establishment of technical standards for content development and sharing. Groups involved in developing learning standards are working together under the umbrella of the federal Advanced Distributed Learning (ADL) initiative. Led by the U.S. Department of Defense, with the cooperation of other federal agencies, academia, the private sector, and the technology industry, this group has developed standards for interoperability known as the Sharable Courseware Object Reference Model (SCORM). These standards provide a foundation for the Pentagon to build the learning environment of the future. The influence of this initiative will reach far beyond the military, as have past initiatives including the development of the Internet.

Similarly, the Schools Interoperability Framework (SIF) is an industry initiative to develop an open specification to ensure that K-12 instructional and administrative software applications can work together. Close to 100 hardware and software companies and school districts are involved in this effort. Their objective is to "revolutionize" the management and accessibility of data within schools and school districts, enabling diverse applications to interact and share data efficiently, reliably, and securely, regardless of platform. Adopting standards such as these makes sharing of content and collaborative design more feasible. For example, the SchoolTone Alliance, a global partnership of over 25 leading education service providers, is developing a framework for web-based portals that build on this model.

The fifth trend is the emergence of "adaptive technology"-technology that combines speech recognition, gesture recognition, text-to-speech conversion, language translation, and sensory immersion to change the very substance of network-enhanced human communication.

A final trend is the dramatic drop in the unit cost of broadband. Bandwidth will decrease in cost and increase in power more rapidly than the advances in chip technology described by Moore's law. Ubiquitous Internet access can become a viable option for all, rather than a privileged few.

These are promising trends. But to benefit fully from these trends, learners must have affordable, easy access to the computing power necessary to bring these resources to the desktop, the laptop, or the appropriate Internet-enabled handheld-or even wearable device.

A number of surveys tracking the growth of computer connections in homes and schools provide a picture of what the U.S. Department of Commerce calls a growing trend toward "digital inclusion." But digital inclusion must work wherever the learner and learning opportunities come together-at home, at school, and on the college campus.

Household Internet Access: In the last two years Internet access in households has grown dramatically. In US, in just a year and a half the share of households with Internet access doubled, rising from 26.2 percent to 41.5 percent. Rural households are catching up. The data show a 75 percent increase in rural household access over this 18 month period, so that today 38.9 percent of rural households have Internet access. Broadband penetration is still greater in central cities (12.2 percent) and urban areas (11.8 percent) than in rural areas (7.3 percent). The national average for households with broadband access is 10.7 percent. But troubling gaps remain and are expanding in some cases:

— Between December 1998 and August 2000 the gap in Internet access between Black households and the national average grew from 15 percent to 18 percent; for Hispanic households the gap grew from 14 percent to 18 percent.

— About a third of the U.S. population uses the Internet at home; only 18.9 percent of Blacks and 16.1 percent of Hispanics do so.

— About 1/3 of the U.S population uses the Internet at home. Only 16.1% of Hispanics and 18.9% of Blacks do.

Home access is important for students doing research, taking online courses, and communicating with teachers and other learners. For parents, online access means new kinds of communication with their children's schools, with their children's teachers, and with other parents. For all households, Internet access is another way to connect with their communities and government services. Home access helps to advance economic opportunities: low-income users were the most likely to report using the Internet to look for jobs.

Wiring Schools and Libraries: Those learners without Internet access at home rely on schools, libraries, and other public places to provide this access. For households with incomes below $40,000, students are more likely to have Internet access at school (31 percent have Internet access at home versus 56 percent at school). For many economically disadvantaged and minority group youngsters, a computer at school or in the library after school is the only link to the wide world of the Internet. Educational institutions are struggling to provide students with Internet access, and great strides have been made in bringing schools, libraries, and postsecondary institutions online. But here again, there are gaps.

The E-rate has been a major factor in providing school and library access. Enacted as a part of the Universal Service Program of the Telecommunications Act of 1996, the E-rate program provides discounts to public and private schools, libraries, and consortia on the costs of telecommunications services, Internet access, and internal networking.

However, E-rate discounts do not reach places where many others could benefit from the learning opportunities of the Internet-from daycare centers to senior centers, and from adult literacy programs and community centers to museums, and other venues for both formal and informal learning.

K-12 Educational Access: The recent growth in Internet connectivity has been dramatic. School connectivity has grown from 65 percent in 1996 to 95 percent in 1999. But what counts most for instructional purposes is classroom connectivity, providing student access to Internet connections where they learn-in the classroom. Classroom connectivity has soared from 14 percent in 1996 to 63 percent in 1999. Classroom access is still greater for the wealthy. Wealthy school classroom access almost doubles that of poor schools. And per computer access is no better: schools with the highest percentage of students in poverty (measured by percentages of students receiving free and reduced price lunches) average 16 students per Internet-linked computer. For wealthy schools the ratio is 7 students per computer, while the national average is 9 to 1. Poor schools need a significant investment to reach the ratio of 4 students per classroom computer considered a minimum level of access for effective use.

Postsecondary Institutions: Postsecondary education institutions are also rapidly expanding student access to the Internet. Yet, there are institutional disparities. For example, 58 percent of all postsecondary students own their own computer. This figure varies from a high of 79 percent of students at private universities, to 34 percent of those attending private two-year institutions, and 39.6 percent of those attending public two-year institutions.

The lower figure for community colleges is particularly troubling because community colleges- with their tradition of low tuition, flexible programming, open door admissions, and customized services-enroll proportionately larger percentages of the postsecondary student population, and larger percentages of minority students. Currently 55 percent of Hispanic-and Native-Americans, and 46 percent of African-American undergraduates, are enrolled in community colleges.

In e-testimony to the Commission, the United Negro College Fund (UNCF) reported that only 15 percent of students attending member institutions had their own computers. They also reported that:

— College students are more than twice as likely to have access to a college-owned computer than their private historically-black colleges and universities counterparts.

— Seventy-four percent of faculty owns their own computer as compared with only half of UNCF faculty. Less than half of UNCF faculty have college-owned computers at their desks.

— The number of network servers at UNCF colleges per 1,000 students is approximately half that of all colleges and universities.

— Seventy-five percent of these servers, hubs, routers, and printers are obsolete or nearly obsolete and need replacement.

— Because so many of these institutions are located in rural areas, they face the additional burden of limited access to high-speed Internet access or other learning resources.

Internet for the disabled: The Internet is a double-edged sword for these learners-it can be a gateway to new opportunities, or a barrier that challenges them even further. Among Americans of all ages, nearly 60 percent of those with a disability have never used a personal computer, compared with 25 percent of those without a disability. Among those with a disability, people who have impaired vision and problems with manual dexterity have even lower rates of Internet access and are less likely to use a computer regularly than those with hearing and mobility problems.

Current laws mandate that recipients of federal funds cannot discriminate on the basis of disability. These laws have been extended to ban discrimination by any state or local government under the Americans with Disabilities Act. Educational institutions receiving federal funds must offer equitable access to technology for all students. With the advent of adaptive technology, equity of access for disabled students is possible. Speech synthesizers and screen access software allow the computer to speak whatever text appears on its monitor, facilitating use for blind users. Audio components and simulcasts can be accompanied by real-time captioning. But not all sites and not all distance-learning programs provide these capabilities.

— Multiple means of representation (e.g., a math concept) in both text and graphic modes, animated science simulations, poetry read aloud by the author, etc.

— Multiple means of expression for the learner (use of text, sound, images, video, and combinations of media as vehicles for expressive literacy through writing, illustrating, speaking, video-making, and drawing).

— Multiple means of engagement to attract the easily bored or the easily distracted learner.

Currently, there are basic design and development guidelines that are widely available and accepted by industry and consumers, through the Web Accessibility Initiative of the World Wide Web Consortium. As a support for Web site developers, the Center for Applied Special Technology (CAST) created Bobby, a Web-based tool that analyzes Web pages for their accessibility to people with disabilities. CAST offers Bobby as a free public service in order to expand opportunities for people with disabilities through the innovative uses of computer technology. Once a Web site receives a Bobby approved rating, it is authorized to display a "Bobby Approved" icon. CAST also maintains a database of Bobby-approved Web sites. Universal designs are those that eliminate "gratuitous barriers" while adding functional equivalents.

These universal design principles ultimately benefit all learners. They support what neuroscience and other learning research have shown us about learning-there is not one "typical" learner, just as there is not one path to learning. Web-based learning environments can provide support and challenge through multiple means of:

— Representation (e.g., a math concept in both text and graphic modes; animated science simulations; poetry read aloud by the author; etc.)

— Expression (i.e., use of text; sound; images; video; and combinations of media as vehicles for expressive literacy through writing, illustrating, speaking, video-making, and drawing)

— Engagement to attract the easily bored or the easily distracted learner

Designing accessibility into an Internet site or a course at the beginning is far less expensive than after the fact. Designs that create barriers harm everyone, not just people with disabilities.

Professional Development

A recent survey by the US National Education Association (NEA) found that most teachers have some facility using computers. Ninety-four percent of NEA members, and 99 percent of those under 35, are able to surf the Web. However, familiarity does not equal proficiency. Most do not know how to apply these skills in classroom instruction. Common sense holds that technology training for teachers will no longer be an issue if we can wait long enough for a new generation of younger teachers, raised on technology, to enter the profession. However, this is one common sense belief that simply does not hold up to close examination.

Another survey found that young teachers' self-assessment of their ability to teach with technology was no different than that of their older colleagues. While younger teachers may have basic technology skills-(e.g., the ability to use word-processing software, spreadsheets, presentation software, and Internet browsers)-they realize that they, like their older colleagues, do not know how to apply these skills to teaching.

The ability to use technology for non-instructional purposes does not necessarily translate into either the will or the capability to use technology to support student learning. Although they are not technophobes, these new teachers lack a clear conception of effective classroom uses of technology in their subject area.

Professional development is the critical ingredient for effective use of technology in the classroom. Seventy percent of educators polled regarding technology in instruction put professional development at the top of their list of technology challenges. They said what is needed is both the initial training for those just beginning to use technology and continuing education to support the growth of innovators. Three consecutive years of surveys in higher education showed the same thing: institutions ranked their greatest technological challenge as "assisting faculty to integrate information technology into instruction."

Professional development is often called "training," but the term implies much more than just building basic technology skills. It means developing a vision built on the understanding that technology is a tool that can offer solutions to longstanding teaching and learning problems. It is more than knowing how to automate past practices. It is the growing understanding that comes with confidence to "think with technology" in order to approach old problems in new ways.

Almost two-thirds of all teachers feel they are not at all prepared or only somewhat well prepared to use technology in their teaching. Change is necessary on two fronts: in the preparatory (pre-service) education of teacher candidates, and in the continuing (in-service) education of those already in the education profession. Both groups need assistance and support in using the best tools technology offers to meet teaching goals and challenges.

Some might wonder why past investments in technology training for K-12 classroom teachers have not had a greater impact. The reality is that the money spent on teacher training with technology is just a fraction of what is needed. In 1995, the Office of Technology Assessment sounded the alarm in a report on teachers and technology, urging that schools and districts devote at least 30 percent of technology budgets to teacher training and support. Yet, of the $4.2 billion that K-12 schools spent on technology in 1996, only 6 percent was for training. This figure is beginning to rise: in the 1999-2000 school year, 17 percent of public school technology spending went to teacher training, according to an annual survey conducted by Market Data Retrieval. Still, this remains far below the mark. Today NEA recommends that schools devote 40 percent of their technology budgets to teacher training.

The training teachers do receive is usually too little, too basic, and too generic to help them develop real facility in teaching with technology. Ninety-six percent reported that the most common training they received was on basic computer skills.

Another survey of public school teachers in US found that while most (78 percent) received some technology-related professional development in the 1998-99 school year, the training was basic and brief, lasting only 1 to 5 hours for 39 percent of teachers, and just 6 to 10 hours for another 19 percent of those trained. Teachers need more than a quick course in basic computer operations. They need guidance in using the best tools in the best ways to support the best kinds of instruction. And they need something more. They need time.

When asked in a National Center for Education Statistics (NCES) survey in US to name the greatest barrier to their use of computers and the Internet in the classroom, most teachers (82 percent) cited lack of "release time" (time outside classroom) to "learn, practice, or plan ways to use computers or the Internet." This factor outweighed their concern about too few computers (78 percent) or lack of time in the schedule for students to use computers in class (80 percent).

Business, for all its pressure to manage the cost of employee time, doesn't operate this way. Once again, the success of the private sector in integrating technology into its operations suggests a better approach for American education. In the business world, training is tailored, focused, and just-in-time. In the education world, it is more often one-size-fits-all, generic, and just-in-case. The overwhelming majority (90 percent) of all corporate and government training occurs on paid time.

In public schools, teachers report just over a third (39 percent) of their professional development occurs on paid time. Professionals in other fields expect to be trained regularly. Motorola, long the standard for industry, provides every employee with at least 40 hours of training each year.

Equally significant, professionals in other fields are provided with follow-up support needed for that training to take root-including immediate access to the hardware and software on which they are trained, Internet connections, and easy access to support personnel and follow- up skill building.

Many teachers have been trained on systems not installed in their schools. Many do not receive follow-up support. Only 67 percent of teachers in the NCES survey reported that follow-up or advanced training was available to them. Most business professionals have personal computers provided to them at work and some industries give employees computers they can use at home. But K-12 teachers rarely are provided these benefits. Although 62 percent of teachers have access to a desktop computer while at school, only 28 percent have the ability to borrow one for occasional use at home.

Most teachers are not rewarded or reimbursed for the time they spend in training. Just as some teachers spend their own money for classroom supplies, some teachers pay for their own preparation. Many take classes on their own time and pay their own tuition or fees. For example, OnlineLearning.net, an online continuing education provider, offered over 1,000 courses in the past year. Over 6,000 teachers enrolled in these courses. Eighty-five percent paid the $450 tuition fee on their own.

Technology training rarely translates directly into higher pay for teachers. In fact, a growing concern among schools is the lure of higher salaries offered in the private sector to teachers and administrators who do exhibit strong technical proficiencies or a desire to develop these.

There are other ways K-12 teachers are treated differently than professionals in business and industry. Intellectual support, as well as technical support, is rare. A recent study in US found that only 13 percent of the US's teachers work in what could be defined as a "high quality technology-supported environment. For most teachers, technical assistance is limited, if available at all.

Another study measuring technology support for district technology coordinators in 27 states found that it took from 14 hours to more than 7 days to fix a technology problem in a school or classroom. The average response time was more than two days. While this would be unthinkable in most businesses, imagine what it means to a teacher who has developed a lesson around the Internet, only to discover that the whole class is disrupted for an unknown period of time. It is simply intolerable. Fewer than 20 percent of all schools have a full-time technology coordinator. In most cases, technology coordinators are charged with training teachers and helping them integrate technology in their classes. In reality, they spend most of their time on technical support. On a weekly basis, full-time technology coordinators spend only 3 to 4 minutes per teacher assisting with technology integration. Part-time technology coordinators perform this kind of assistance only 1 to 2 minutes per week.

But the larger problem is one that is endemic to the K-12 teaching profession-the isolation of the classroom teacher. How can Internet access change that? Most of a teacher's day is spent separated from colleagues, with little time or opportunity to share in the give-and-take of problem-solving common in most office or work environments. For elementary and secondary education teachers, planning periods are few and often occur in isolation. Group meetings are focused on issues that affect the institution as a whole or the department or grade level, but they don't offer the opportunity to express the concerns or share the wisdom of the individual teacher.

Teachers rarely have the opportunity to work with others to share their questions, concerns, and successes. Most are isolated and, unlike other professionals, have little access to the resources they need to stay up to date in their fields. In contrast, teachers in other countries are provided far more paid time for planning: Japanese teachers spend about 40 percent of their paid time on professional development and collaboration compared with about 14 percent for their American counterparts.

Internet as a Teaching Tool: The Internet is making it possible to connect teachers to each other, giving opportunities for mentoring, collaboration, and formal and informal online learning. Traditional one-size-fits-all professional development workshops are giving way to a new, more teacher-centered, self-directed model of teacher learning. Through the Internet, teachers have access to high quality online professional development opportunities beyond what the local school or district is able to offer.

Online courses and seminars, follow-up consultations and mentoring, and collaborations with experts and peers can take place without the expense and classroom disruption created by repeated absences for face-to-face meetings. And, in working in online environments, teachers obtain a collateral benefit: they learn important technological skills.

A supportive social structure is one of the key elements for successful online learning. In projects like SRI International's TAPPED IN program, supported by the National Science Foundation, the technological tools and communication resources serve as the underpinnings of a well-maintained community of practitioners. Those wishing to create their own projects are assisted by TAPPED IN support personnel.

User groups include school districts, museums, and teacher education programs. Through TAPPED IN, educators can participate in online courses, take their own students online, experiment with new ways to teach or conduct research, or participate in community-wide events. Since opening in 1997, TAPPED IN has served more than 9,000 K-12 teachers, librarians, researchers, teacher education faculty, professional development staff, and other education professionals.

But unless new teachers enter the classroom ready to teach with technology, we will never catch up. If teacher education programs do not address this issue head on, we will lose the opportunity to get it right with a whole generation of new teachers-and the students they teach. The size of the challenge is staggering. There are three million teachers in K-12 schools today. In the next decade alone, we must recruit and train two million more new teachers just to replace retirees and to meet expected growth in enrolment. Put another way, one-third of today's teachers have 20 years or more of teaching experience; two-thirds are in mid-career. As the teacher population ages, moving into retirement, 54.2 million students are expected in K-12 education by 2009, up 2 million from 1997. There is the need of a fundamental change in recruiting new teachers, and giving them the tools to do a more effective job.

In the midst of this crisis, teacher education has yet to come to grips with the immediacy of preparing a new generation of teachers to use technology as a teaching tool. Teacher education programs tend to be profit centers for colleges and universities-they pay for themselves with strong and steady student enrollments and have few of the expenses associated with equipping science laboratories, engineering, or other professional programs.

As noted in a 1999 report on teacher preparation by the CEO Forum on Education and Technology, many teacher education programs "receive less attention than the higher status professional programs in the university such as law, engineering, business, and medicine have a less affluent alumni base, meaning that large gifts from donors are harder to obtain. The most recent Campus Computing Project survey asked chief technology officers (CTOs) of higher education institutions to compare the information technology components in departmental programs across their campuses. Overall, the CTOs ranked their campus' education programs eighth of 10 in use of the Internet and Web resources, seventh in the use of technology for instruction, and tied for sixth in preparing their students with the technology skills needed over the next decade. Most teacher education institutions now offer what is called "the course" in information technology. But providing a stand-alone course about technology is not the same as ensuring that courses in teaching methods integrate technology as a way of building understanding or assessing learning.

Faculty in teacher education programs, many of whom were educated and taught in schools before computers were a part of the educational landscape, are not comfortable or skilled in teaching with technology. This problem extends across the college experience of teacher candidates. If they do not see their faculty use technology in the courses they take outside their teaching major, tomorrow's teachers will not have a full understanding of how technology advances understanding in each academic area.

It is clear that the need for professional development in technology among higher education faculty parallels that required by educators in K-12 schools. It is also clear that campus higher education leaders have a deep responsibility for modernizing their colleges of education and incorporating a priority on teaching and learning with technology.

There are, of course, exceptions and promising new practices that suggest change is coming. These include leadership initiatives undertaken by Congress, the states, universities, professional organizations, and the business community.

— The Higher Education Act Amendments, passed by Congress and signed into law in 1998, provide a gateway for technology integration in college teacher education programs. A major objective within the section of the Act focusing on enhancing the quality of teaching in the U.S. is to "hold institutions of higher education accountable for preparing teachers who have the necessary teaching skills and are highly competent in the academic content areas in which the teachers plan to teach, such as mathematics, science, English, foreign languages, history, economics, art, civics, Government, and geography, including training in the effective uses of technology in the classroom..."

— An increasing number of states now require teachers to demonstrate proficiency in technology as one component for receiving certification. However, only 4 require technology training for re-certification.

— The US National Council for Accreditation of Teacher Education (NCATE), the largest accreditation association of schools, colleges, and departments of education, has made technology an area of accreditation focus. While this is an important leadership message, only 38 percent of the US's 1,300 teacher preparation programs are accredited by NCATE. Many schools, colleges, and departments of education choose not to apply to NCATE; others have been unable to meet its standards.

— The CEO Forum developed a special STaR (School Technology and Readiness) self-assessment tool for schools and colleges of education. At the urging of Education Secretary Richard Riley and President Bill Clinton in May 2000, 243 institutions have "taken the pledge" to conduct self-assessments as a first step for turning their programs around and moving from "early tech" or "developing tech" to "advanced tech" or "target tech."

New funding initiatives have also led to promising practices. The US National Science Foundation-supported "Inquiry Learning Forum" is a model of using the Internet for teacher growth. The U.S. Department of Education's Preparing Tomorrow's Teachers with Technology (PT3) Program, begun in 1999, is bringing new ideas, new collaborations, and new models to teacher education. The PT3 program has made $150 million in federal funding available to 352 teacher preparation institutions to help them develop capacity, implement new programs, and provide innovative catalysts for broader change. These programs are just beginning to take root, but they offer promise for the future.

Many teachers lack connections to colleagues with similar interests, responsibilities, and challenges. Imagine being the only physics teacher in a school. Under normal school conditions, you could go for weeks or months without contact with another physics teacher. Sharing teaching strategies and content with colleagues or even getting outside advice or constructive criticism-this just isn't a part of your world.

No wonder so many teachers feel professionally isolated. Four hundred teachers in Indiana are turning to a new online environment, the Inquiry Learning Forum (ILF), to establish connections with other teachers, as well as to expand access to classroom resources. They are acting to end the isolation of teachers.

The ILF is a video centered, web-based learning forum designed to support an online community of current and future science and mathematics teachers interested in "inquiry-based" teaching. The ILF provides opportunities to virtually "visit" classrooms across Indiana. It features a large video library of classroom episodes and enables teachers to discuss, annotate, reflect upon, and replay these classroom episodes as needed.

The home screen of the ILF, shown here, displays which of the classrooms are available through the Visit Classrooms space. When ILF members select a specific classroom lesson, they can view a videotape of that lesson being implemented. They can also review a lesson overview, reflective commentary, descriptions of teaching activity, lesson plans, students' examples. In addition to the Visit Classroom spaces, there are also 5 other virtual spaces designed to support professional development needs. The ILF Office is the place where new participants can secure a password, get help with technology, or make suggestions. The Workroom provides groups with an online space to form working circles, or sub-communities, that facilitate collaboration on a particular project, product, or goal.

The Lounge hosts general conferences that are not tied to a particular classroom as well as a space for real-time chat to allow users to communicate with others. The Auditorium is the place where special events can occur. These usually involve chat discussions with a white board and resources. It also provides the opportunity for video-casting live or recorded presentations for discussion. Any member of the community can hold a workshop, experts can be brought in, or there may be simultaneous discussion of specific issues.

The Library is a place where teachers can go to access reference materials of interest, including references on teaching resource materials, grants, applied research and theory, state initiatives, and other materials the teachers identify as relevant. Finally, My Desk is the place where a teacher can store bookmarks to resources and classrooms of personal interest. Not only do teachers have the opportunity to share lesson plans, unit plans, and other resources through the ILF, they are also able to watch other teachers implement these resources in their classrooms, read the personal reflections of these teachers, and discuss what they have seen, heard, or read. Every classroom resource available in the ILF community is "attached" to a videotaped segment of a lesson or a particular discussion thread. This enables teachers to not only find resources, but also to read or hear about how they might be used in a particular classroom.

Classroom computer stations equipped with small cameras, audio, electronic notebook software, and annotation tools provide HCRHS student writers with live communications links with university student mentors at Rider University. The high school students meet weekly with these university mentors to discuss manuscripts in a lively, re-imagined, electronic version of the traditional writing workshop. Feedback is immediate and focused. The university student mentors, who receive English credit for the supervised interaction, grow with the high school writers.

Research Development

Educational research, focused on using long-term, longitudinal studies as well as aggregated short-term trials supported by technology, should be directed at enhancing performance in learning. We know that technology offers both the impetus and the opportunity to vastly improve learning performance. Without a vigorous, dynamic research base, however, we will miss the opportunity to advance the state of the art and science of education.

Educational research suffers from three major problems:

— Not enough money is spent on educational research

— Educational research often does not support enhanced learning performance

— Educational research often is not accessible to teachers or easily translated into practice.

In its 1997 landmark report, the Panel on Educational Technology of the President's Committee of Advisors on Science and Technology (PCAST) recommended that "the federal government initiate a large-scale program of rigorous empirical research aimed at improving both the effectiveness and the cost-effectiveness of elementary and secondary education in the United States ... at a level equal to at least 0.5 percent of the US's aggregate K-12 educational spending, or approximately $1.5 billion per year at present expenditure levels."

Even adding the $60 million spent by the Research, Evaluation, and Communication Division of the US National Science Foundation's Education and Human Resources Directorate, best estimates suggest total spending for education research is in the $600 million range.

The federal government invests more than $75 billion a year in research in science and technology development in military, health, aerospace, agriculture, and other areas. Added to this are equivalent industry investments. It is obvious that R & D in these fields are mature. By comparison, the learning R & D field is in its infancy.

As reported in recent US Academy of Sciences reports, learning sciences have made substantial progress in the past 30 years, more than most people realize. This expanding knowledge base about how we learn has important implications for improving education at all levels. Learning environments should be centered around knowledge, learners, social interactions, and assessment. Instead, learning environments in school often:

— Focus on the short-term recall of facts, rather than opportunities for deeper building of knowledge

— Organize around the top-down, teacher-and-textbook centered instruction, rather than the needs of the individual learner

— Limit social interaction to occasional times with peers in the classroom encouraging solo study, rather than collaboration

— Allow current assessment to influence instruction in ways that may not match the goals of 21st Century learning.

Schools often use technology to mimic this pattern of a top-down, lecture or text-driven model of instruction. Similarly, we have used the Internet in a narrow fashion, like vast textbooks or lectures online, instead of exploring its interactive potential. Technology can support what we now know to be more effective learning environments.

Interactive applications linked to the Internet can provide environments better matched to support learner-centered, knowledge-centered, community-centered, and assessment-centered conditions for learning. New technological tools and applications allow for expanded forms of communication, analysis, and expression by students and teachers. These innovations support new forms of teaching and understanding built on the early findings of learning research.

Perhaps the greatest barrier to innovative teaching is assessment that measures yesterday's learning goals. It is a classic dilemma: tests do a good job of measuring basic skills, which, in turn, influence the teaching of these skills so students can score well on the tests.

Testing works well so long as we are testing the right things. Learning frameworks at the K-12 level are important for providing a common definition of what is valued, but often they are built around collections of content rather than demonstrations of higher-order cognitive, affective, and social skills vital in a knowledge-based economy. Most states use standardized tests for determining how well students meet these frameworks at several grade levels.

Witnesses before the Commission made it clear that academic standards are important, but they must be connected to the needs of the 21st Century. Often this is not the case. Too often today's tests measure yesterday's skills with yesterdays' testing technologies-paper and pencil. What will it take to develop tests that truly reflect what students need to learn for the 21 st Century? It will take a concerted effort and large amounts of R & D funding with the collaboration of educators and psychometricians, content specialists, and technologists.

Above all, it will take a focus on the potential of technology to help us better measure the knowledge, competencies, and understandings we value in education. The same kinds of innovative 21 st Century tools and learning environments that people are developing for teaching and learning can be designed to administer and score student performances.

Advances in testing technologies have made it possible to extend test item formats beyond the selected-response formats of past test designs. For example, through web-based testing a student may be asked to place works of art along a timeline, to design a building to meet a set of constraints, to troubleshoot a faulty system, or to analyze a text and compare it for historical accuracy with other documents of the same era. In computer adaptive testing, the test "adapts" to the examinee's performance on it.

The individual is given a question, and, if answered correctly, moves on to more difficult questions. Incorrect responses generate less difficult questions. Information is stored on the computer and the score reflects the skill level he or she has achieved. The use of computer-adaptive testing is growing in the military and training fields, and for professional certification and graduate admissions testing.

With storage and delivery capabilities of the Web, it is now possible to provide web-based test administration. A central server may contain an "item bank" of thousands of questions of varying types and difficulty levels.

Students could take the tests from their classroom or computer lab, with the delivery of items adapted to the students' performance.

Scoring could be immediate, and administrators and teachers could have access to this information at any level- aggregated by school, grade level, classroom, individual student, or even concept area. This feedback could provide much better monitoring of achievement at all levels, and, unlike today's large-scale assessments, make it possible for teachers to adapt instruction in response to commonly found difficulties, or an individual student's learning profile.

The use of information technologies, for both teaching and assessment, afford new opportunities for an increased focus on the application of knowledge, not just its rote recitation. Assessment of student performance can be embedded, almost seamlessly, in systems that promote continuous learning.

However, the current forms of testing are not designed to measure how educational reforms, including those based on technology, can improve student understanding. This mismatch between reforms and testing leads many to underestimate the impact of technology. It discourages educators from spending the effort to undertake these reforms and changes in practice. Fortunately, development of sophisticated test construction, delivery, and scoring through new technologies will make it possible to do a better job of evaluating the skills we seek to build.

Too often educational research has been seen as esoteric, faddish, or too far from the realm of the day-to-day to have meaning. It takes too long, and is too little used. In part, this reflects the isolated researcher in the university community who may not be connected with K-12 schools, or even the teacher education programs in his or her own institution.

The highest forms of knowledge-building today are those that come through collaboration and sharing of what is known, just as medical research pulls together relevant specialties in exploring a problem and potential ways of addressing it. Similarly, research on learning will need to draw on specialists in neurocognition, behavioral and biological sciences, and other fields, as well as the expertise of content area specialists, educational practitioners, designers, and technology developers to create the applications that carry research findings into the classroom.

Teachers can now be more a part of the process, as the Internet links them to the world of the researcher, making classrooms more likely settings for research and for implementation of research findings. Witnesses before this Commission called for such "mission-oriented" research, combining basic and applied research, designed to yield fundamental new knowledge while exploring problems that have important practical consequences. And this research should focus on problems of practice faced daily by teachers and administrators-research for real-time practice, not just research on practice.

Imagine if schools, on demand, could apply research technologies to profile what a student needs to learn, how he or she learns best, what his or her learning style is, and what worked or did not work in the past, with continuous feedback to teachers, parents, and the student. The Internet, with its tools for collaborative research and immediate communication, makes it possible to create new models of knowledge- building communities that can support and quickly implement new forms of research, innovation, and application.

Learning over the Web can minimize the impact of disabilities by eliminating transportation barriers. It can allow students to reveal their disabilities at their discretion. It can promote equality among learners, with and without disabilities, reducing potential discrimination. And it can make previously inaccessible classroom materials accessible.

People who are blind, deaf, or who have mobility impairments can overcome numerous educational and vocational barriers if online educational materials are produced in a way that makes them accessible. Techniques and technologies are already in place for assuring such accessibility. What is missing is public awareness of these standards and policies to guarantee that they are followed. A powerful example of accessible design can be found in the new web-based multimedia physics curriculum called "Physics Interactive Video Tutor" (PIVoT) created by the Massachusetts Institute of Technology (MIT). PIVoT is designed to provide freshman students with a virtual learning environment that offers the immediacy, responsiveness, and dynamism of a traditional tutor.

As part of PIVoT's activities, the Corporation for Public Broadcasting/WGBH National Center for Accessible Media (NCAM) of US is collaborating with MIT on a three-year project funded by the Science Foundation and the Mitsubishi Electric America Foundation. Launched in January 2000, this project is using PIVoT as a model to test, implement, document, and promote the development of multimedia access solutions that will make distance-learning accessible to blind, low-vision, deaf, and hard-of-hearing students. To understand the PIVoT approach, it is important to first understand why so much web-based material is difficult for disabled students to access.

Web browsers present information through software known as a graphical user interface (GUI). Navigation through GUIs is difficult for blind and visually impaired people because image maps, buttons, menus, and other controls are often invisible or nameless when accessed by a blind user's assistive technology, such as a screen reader or refreshable Braille display. Access to most graphical content must be provided via technical instructions known as "alt-text tags." The PIVoT web site is becoming a model of accessible Web site design and is striving for adherence to the Web Content Accessibility Guidelines of the World Wide Web Consortium's Web (W3C) Accessibility Initiative.

PIVoT supports disabled users in the following ways:

First, it offers better design and layout. NCAM is working with PIVoT designers to improve the Web site's layout so that blind users can more easily navigate the site. For example, designers have improved text/ background contrast to help visually impaired students use the site more effectively.

Second, it offers access to tables. Reading and manipulating tables is an important way of processing scientific information-but tables present a particular problem for blind users. Tables require that the user refer to both row and column headings in order to interpret the information in a single cell. The PIVoT Web site is being designed to permit blind users to explore a set of tabular data more efficiently through cues that help them understand these relationships.

Third, it offers access to math equations. Improving access to equations and graphs is crucial in making math and science accessible to blind and visually impaired students. A promising standard is the MathML specification from the W3C. A discussion is underway regarding appropriate MathML browsers in conjunction with the User Agents Working Group of the Web Accessibility Initiative. Once tools are available for authoring MathML, the PIVoT project intends to use them to prepare physics materials for the Web. This solution should enable blind students to read and manipulate equations with output in speech and Braille.

Fourth, it offers access to multimedia. The MIT development team has elected to use the W3C's Synchronized Multimedia Integration Language (SMIL) to assemble and present the course's multimedia lectures and help files.

NCAM's caption-authoring tool, the Media Access Generator (MAGpie), is being used in the PIVoT project to add captions to multimedia, thus simplifying the process of making these clips accessible to deaf and hard-of-hearing students. MAGpie can also sequence audio descriptions into SMIL presentations, making them more accessible to blind or visually impaired students. When implemented from the start, accessibility features such as alt-text tags, captions, audio descriptions, and proper layout add little if anything to the cost of a Web site.

However, when implemented as add-ons, after the site has been launched, considerable costs related to labour and time may be incurred as the site is retrofitted to accommodate specific features. It is important to consider that accessibility improvements benefit all users, not just those who are disabled. For example, Web users who are not sight-impaired may turn off their browser's automatic image-loading feature to make use of alt-text tags to identify and manipulate images.

All users have the option of using captioned multimedia when viewing movie clips in a noisy environment, or where the use of sound is not appropriate. Caption (text) tracks are also useful as indices for searching through large collections of digital video files-the captions act as keywords. Within three years, the PIVoT project aims to:

— Enable science-focused high school and college students who are blind, visually-impaired, deaf, or hard-of-hearing to participate in an innovative and challenging web-based introductory physics curriculum

— Provide developers, publishers, and distributors of distance-learning and educational multimedia with recommended practices and an applied demonstration of accessible design principles for network-delivered multimedia

— Enable the MIT Center for Advanced Educational Services 4 to institutionalize the technical capabilities developed through this project to develop a range of future educational products that are accessible to individuals with disabilities.

Through the application of pragmatic and common sense design and development standards it is possible to provide the enormous benefits of accessible online learning equally to all students. While educators and policymakers talk about e-learning, the medical profession is doing it.

The Online Content

The real revolution now taking place is not the hardware of technology, but the intellectual technology of information, communication, and the augmentation of human intelligence. All too often, discussions about web-based learning tend to fall back on a simplistic faith in the power of technology. Of course interactivity is a powerful draw for teachers and students alike. But dazzling technology has no meaning unless it supports content that meets the needs of learners. Some of the content currently available on the Web is excellent, but much of it is mediocre.

Challenges await content developers and educators in producing, distributing, cataloging, indexing, and evaluating good online content. They must address gaps in this market, find ways to build fragmented lesson plans into full courses, fully develop the promise of postsecondary educational opportunities on the Web, and assure quality in this new environment.

The educational content market is a huge business. Total U.S. spending each year on textbooks and instructional technology content amounts to approximately $4 billion. Online content currently represents only a fraction of that market, although many expect the Internet to both capture a large share from offline content sources, such as textbooks, as well as expand the size of this market overall. According to one report, 13 percent of K-12 schools already subscribe to online curriculum.

Traditional content providers-publishers and software developers-are increasingly joined by new providers of online content. Federal agencies, museums, teachers, and even students themselves are contributing to web-based content. Much of the online content consists of data, Web pages, applets, and other information that teachers use as supplements to text-based teaching, rather than full courses. For example, the U.S. Department of Education sponsors the Gateway to Educational Materials, containing more than 14,000 lesson ideas and learning resources from over 200 organizations.

Many private-sector providers have changed their focus from producing content to aggregating instructional information, acting as a "portal" or access point for other content-based resources and information provided by teachers and schools. For example, bigchalk.com aggregates "best of class" content and makes it available to subscribing schools through community Web sites.

However, only a handful of providers have been able to take advantage of the online education content market. That is because the market is highly fragmented (products and services are targeted by age, grade, and subject matter and marketed to over 15,000 school districts) and often finite. The cost to compete in these specialized sub-markets is high, forcing many providers to retreat and instead produce "big ticket" general studies content that historically have provided a greater rate of return.

School districts and states may soon be faced with a paradox. Overall market growth, along with expansion of the delivery mechanism, may not, by themselves, be enough to sustain robust competition and innovation in product design, capability, and customization. Unless school districts and states create significant demand for innovative online learning materials, it may not be economically feasible for many online education content providers to stay in the business. The result could be a latter-day online equivalent to the current K-12 textbook market-domination by just a few providers, limited choice, and perhaps, stagnancy in innovation and design. The good news, however, is that some states are beginning to respond by investing in approaches that provide web-based content for educators, when and where they need it.

The Massachusetts' Virtual Education Space (VES), for example, will provide every K-12 student, teacher, and parent a personal "workspace" they can log onto with an Internet browser and personal password. Students will have access to assignments, content linked to their specific learning objectives, works-in-progress, and portfolios of completed work.

Teachers will be able to access state and district curriculum standards related to their teaching areas, and a database of content and lesson plans linked to the standards. Collaboration, planning, administration, and assessment tools will also be at the teacher's access. Parents, too, can access their children's assignments, work to date, and teacher evaluations of progress.

Washington State is partnering with Massachusetts, developing its own version of this program called WAVES. Several other states are discussing working together in development of similar "smart desktops". Some school districts have developed their own instructional management systems that use the Web to help teachers organize and manage instruction more effectively and efficiently. Fairfax County Public Schools in Virginia testified that it is investing upwards of $100,000 to develop several web-based high school courses for its students. PreK-12: Moving From Online

Materials, to Courses, to Full Programs While there are thousands of online lesson plans and supplementary course materials at the preK-12 level, full courses are more limited. Most have been developed by state, district, or cross-regional online high schools.

State-created online high schools offer courses that parallel those required in the traditional high school curriculum of the state. As more states are developing virtual high schools, a greater range of courses are being offered online. Another model is the Virtual High School (VHS) Project funded through a U.S. Department of Education Challenge Grant to the Hudson, Massachusetts School District and operated by the Concord Consortium. VHS offers over 156 courses to about 250 schools in 32 states and 13 countries. Many of these courses are taken as electives rather than core curriculum requirements.

At VHS, the per student tuition fee can be waived if a school creates an online course or facilitates a section of a course that students in any participating school can take. Course design is structured around VHS guidelines and practices taught to teachers through their required participation in the yearlong VHS teacher developer course. Advanced Placement (AP) courses are an important gateway helping to prepare students for college. Many schools do not have either the in-house expertise or enough students to warrant hiring a teacher to offer advanced placement courses.

Today only 60 percent of high schools offer AP courses, with the average high school offering only about 5 AP courses out of 32 subject areas.

A private sector provider, APEX Learning, is providing courses in 10 AP subjects online, as well as other services like AP preparatory materials online.

Evaluation of preK-12 online courses follows the model of traditional education. That is, these courses are certified by the home state or regional accrediting body with jurisdiction in that state. This task becomes considerably more complicated in the case of courses offered across state lines.

Assessment requirements, teacher credentialing, and the granting of credits have all been areas of individual state policy. This means that an offering entity may have to traverse a complex maze of accreditation standards that can vary from state to state.

At the postsecondary level, there is a growing use of online content and tools for both traditional courses and those taken at a distance. Nearly 40 percent of all college classes used Internet resources as part of the syllabus in 1999, compared with 15 percent in 1996. More than 25 percent of all college courses have a Web page compared with 9.2 percent in 1996. Three-fifths (59.3 percent) of all college courses now utilize electronic mail, up from 54.0 percent last year, 44.0 percent in 1998, and 20.1 percent in 1995.

Similarly, two-fifths (42.7 percent) of college courses now use Web resources as a course component, up from 10.9 percent in 1995, 33.1 percent in 1998, and 38.9 percent in 1999. The legacy of the one-room schoolhouse is holding back the potential of the one-world classroom. The regulations that govern much of education today, from pre-kindergarten to higher education, are focused on supporting the welfare of the educational institution, not the individual learner. They were written for an earlier model, the factory model of education in which the teacher is the center of all instruction and all learners must advance at the same rate, despite their varying needs or abilities. Students in this model are expected to spend 7 years in K-6 schooling, another 6 in secondary schools, 2 years in earning an associate's degree or 4 for a bachelor's. Graduate programs have their own inflexible number of credits, courses, and years at one institution as the required rite of passage. Funding follows this progression, and is based on the time a student spends in class and the location of that student and that educational program.

Estimates for school construction, educational services, and materials are built on these time-fixed and place-based models of yesterday. These regulations and requirements no longer match today's realities. High school students can take courses offered online, at their own schedule, and complete them when they pass the appropriate tests. According to some estimates, only 16 percent of today's college students meet the old stereotype of attending full-time, enrolling right after high school, and living on campus.

Course content comes not just from a textbook or materials passed out in class by the teacher, but from many sources, in many formats, and even created by the students themselves. Time, institution, and location do not form the defining elements of education. If not changed, yesterday's regulations will inhibit the potential for new learning opportunities for a new generation of students of all ages.

Regulations to e-Learning

Educational content and services at the elementary, secondary, and higher education levels are increasingly delivered across US. The regulatory schemes of 56 operational units are "dramatically different, ranging from the extremely prescriptive to minimal and in isolated cases non-existent. The pre-kindergarten-grade 12 schools in US face regulation from the federal and local levels, as well as the states. They are subject to countless administrative procedures implemented in an age that predated the Web; many of these procedures cannot accommodate the Internet's agility. School leaders are increasingly confronted by a desire to innovate but are unable to overcome the timeworn rules that dictate the school day, year, delivery systems, and accounting requirements. The Commission received testimony on a wide range of specific concerns. Witnesses cited: Credit policies including the difficulty of transferring and accepting credit across district and state lines and the problem of aligning curriculum standards from one state to another.

Financing policies involving inflexible state budgeting processes, the inability to redirect resources to support distance learning on a per student basis, and less than adequate funding to support the online learning endeavor. Quality assurance issues that address a need to reform state licensing and approval processes to better access the educational value of content and courses available online.

Attendance policies that set the number of hours and days in the classroom as defining measures of achievement alongside other indicators of academic progress. Teacher certification policies that prohibit the transfer of credentials from state to state, thereby inhibiting the growth of online delivery of instruction beyond state lines and creating disincentives to develop new online learning models.

Teacher-student ratio requirements that may not take into account the ability of web-based learning to individualize instruction. Staff compensation requirements that are formulated around 10-month agrarian-model contracts. Accounting procedures that restrict the use of funding to support web-based instruction based on structural rigidity, rather than academic integrity.

The amount and type of postsecondary regulatory oversight at both the state and federal levels varies depending upon the type of institution: for-profit institutions (often called "pro-prietary") are the most highly regulated, followed by non-profit institutions ("independent"), and public (state or local) institutions. For the purposes of state law, an out-of-state public institution is generally treated as an independent or, in some cases, a proprietary institution.

Depending upon where they operate and the kind of programs offered, institutions face a variety of regulatory requirements. Independent institutions generally are regulated by regional accrediting agencies while proprietary schools often fall under the purview of other regulatory bodies. For example, proprietary schools in Texas are regulated by the Texas Workforce Commission rather than the Texas Higher Education Coordinating Board.

Similarly, proprietary schools in California are regulated by the Department of Consumer Affairs, not the California Department of Education. While there are strong reasons for this multifaceted control of education, they often do not apply in an environment characterized by borderless educational opportunities. This challenge was recognized in the 1980s when telecommunications technology meant that broadcast and cable television could be used to deliver "telecourses" across jurisdictional lines.

At that time the State Higher Education Executive Officers Association and the Council on Postsecondary Accreditation created Project ALLTEL (Authorization and Licensure of Learning via Telecommunications). The goal was to create a framework for the regulation of what was that era's distance learning challenge: a proliferation of telecourses of varying levels of quality.

The aim was to set up a system in which states would accept the review of the accreditor of the state where the offering institution was located. The effort failed when states could not agree on a common regulatory framework. There are unintended and unanticipated consequences of this complex nest of rules and regulations:

— Some state requirements are mutually exclusive, making it potentially impossible or impractical to create and adjust web-based programs that meet varying state requirements.

— A program may be forced to meet the lowest common denominator to achieve homogeneity requirements.

— Institutions in one state may refuse to accept credentials awarded by institutions in other states.

— Student aid eligibility may be limited for some students involved in technology- mediated learning.

Beyond the institutional concerns, there are additional barriers for learners. The Internet now makes it possible for a student to purchase a course from his or her local university around the corner, or an institution half a world away. But the same course can be priced very differently. "In-state versus out-of-state tuition rates, non-profit designation, non-profits spinning out for-profits, and for-profit companies create a web of cost structures and tuition regulations that prevent students from choosing the curriculum and price that best meet their needs." This same maze makes it difficult for students to transfer credits from one institution to another and to create the personalized programs that also best meet their needs.

The Internet allows for a learner-centered environment, but the legal and regulatory framework has not adjusted to these changes. "Law is by its nature a slow and deliberative process, and the closer its orbit comes to the development and use of technologies that are changing rapidly, the more likely its impact will be unintended."

The federal government has struggled to establish within statute and regulations a framework that accommodates the promise of the Internet for postsecondary education while promoting access and ensuring accountability. The effort has had mixed results. Three specific federal issues were brought to the Commission's attention: the "12-hour rule," the "50 percent rule," and the federal prohibition on providing incentive compensation in college admissions.

When Congress amended the Higher Education Act in 1992, it added a specific definition of an academic year that prescribed at least 30 weeks of instructional time. Full-time undergraduate students in traditional academic programs are expected to complete at least 24 semester hours or trimester hours (or 36 quarter hours, or 900 clock hours) in that time period to be eligible for the maximum amount of financial aid under the Title IV program. However, the law was silent on establishing an academic workload requirement for students enrolled in Title IV eligible programs offered in a nontraditional time segment.

To deal with this, the U.S. Department of Education developed regulations to implement the statutory definition of an academic year, including establishing full-time workload requirements for students enrolled in programs offered in nontraditional time segments. In 1994, the Department issued formal regulations defining a week of instructional time to mean 12 hours of "regularly scheduled instruction, examinations, or preparation for examination" for programs that are not offered in standard terms.

The 50 Percent Rule Likewise, the "50 percent rule" requires Title IV-eligible institutions to offer at least 50 percent of their instruction in a classroom-based environment. The basis of this rule is to assure that a student is physically participating in an academic course of study for which he or she is receiving federal student financial assistance.

In enacting this provision in the 1992 Higher Education Amendments, Congress sought to address concerns about fraud and abuse within the correspondence school industry. While understanding that physical seat time may not be an appropriate measure of quality for the increasing proliferation of online distance learning programs, the Department views these two rules as important measures of accountability that should not be eliminated or replaced unless there is a viable alternative.

In recent months, public, independent, and proprietary colleges and universities have called for the elimination of the 12-hour rule and the 50 percent rule or, at minimum, a moratorium on their enforcement. These institutions argue that the rules simply don't make sense in light of online distance education and the growing use of the Internet for instructional delivery.

The practical impact is a system of federal student financial assistance that gives substantial preference to the mainstream educational experience. In seeking correctly to halt abuse in the student financial aid program, these rules may, in fact, have the unintended effect of curtailing educational opportunity among thousands who seek financial aid for college, but who do not otherwise fit into the mainstream definition of a college student. Consider these statistics:

— The span from 1970 to 1993 saw a 235 percent growth in students over age 40.

— Over the same time period, the traditional college student cohort increased by 35 percent.

— Forty percent of these students received financial aid, as opposed to only 17 percent of undergraduates over the age of 40.

The U.S. Department of Education is beginning to identify potential alternatives to providing student aid to those enrolled in online programs. In October 2000, it convened dozens of representatives of traditional and nontraditional postsecondary institutions, higher education associations, and the student financial aid sector to address alternatives to the 12-hour rule. The Department's position has been that a wholesale elimination of these rules would leave the door wide open for abuse-and the history of the Title IV program has been marked with such episodes. Instead, the Department is seeking to identify alternatives to current regulation, and assess whether or not they may be more appropriate than current seat-time measures. The Department holds strongly to the belief, however, that rules of some kind are necessary under any circumstance. Institutions take a different position.

Many question the need for the Department to be involved on the regulatory side at all since these institutions already are subject to two sets of quality controls: approval for participation in the Title IV program and accreditation and licensure. They argue that if the problem is with accrediting agencies that are not organized to assess quality effectively in an online learning setting, the answer is to reform the accreditation process, not add another enforcement layer upon postsecondary institutions.

The Department is hosting several working groups with the higher education community to focus on student aid funding for online programs, alternative input and output measures of online quality, and the role of accreditation in assuring academic integrity in the Title IV program. A result could be a statement of the problem and potential alternatives to be considered by Congress and/or Department regulators.

This program exempts 15 institutions and consortia of institutions from the different rules and regulations limiting student financial aid for online postsecondary learners. The goal is to encourage distance education providers to experiment with alternative measurements of online quality and gather data on the success of these alternatives. The results will be presented to Congress along with any proposed changes the Department recommends in this area. Ban on Incentive Compensation Plans In 1992, Congress prohibited colleges and universities that participate in the federal student financial aid program from paying any commission, bonus, or other incentive payments to third party entities based directly or indirectly on their success in helping to secure enrolment of students.

The provision was enacted to protect students against abusive recruiting tactics, although the law is now being interpreted to apply to the enrolment of students via "Web portals." These online "Yellow Pages" are commonly financed through the use of referral fees and tuition-sharing agreements.

Although not the original intent, the language of this restriction effectively bars higher education institutions that participate in Title IV from using third-party Web portals to provide prospective students with access to information about many institutions or provide the same services as institutions offer on their own Web sites-that is, information and application processing.

Current federal regulations permit an institution to use its own Web site to recruit students. However, if the institution pays a Web portal to provide the same passive, asynchronous service, and that payment is based on the number of prospective students visiting the site who ultimately apply or enroll, the institution is at risk of losing its Title IV eligibility. Higher education groups have asked the Department to consider changing regulatory language, reflecting the growing reliance of higher education consumers on Web portals.

However, the Department has concluded that this provision could only be changed through new legislation.

Copyright Protection: Horse and Buggies on the Information Superhighway "The primary objective of copyright is not to reward the labour of authors, but [t]o promote the Progress of Science and useful Arts. To this end, copyright assures authors the right to their original expression, but encourages others to build freely upon the ideas and information conveyed by a work. This result is neither unfair nor unfortunate. It is the means by which copyright advances the progress of science and art."

In a digital age, the organization of data and editorial function of summarizing, hyperlinking, and relating diverse sources of data to meet specific ad hoc needs adds value to content, and represents an emerging class of intellectual capital that goes beyond the concept of 'derivative works' or similar earlier classifications . . . The Internet turns 'consumption' of electronic media into a Breeder Reactor scenario for knowledge building. Effective use of these materials results in additional fuel to power learning in the classroom."

Copyright law serves to balance the legitimate intellectual property rights of authors, publishers, and other copyright owners with society's right to the free exchange of ideas. The Copyright Act of 1976 established principles that make it possible for researchers, students, and members of the public to benefit from access to published information. That access is supported by the concept of "fair use," the provision to reproduce materials under certain circumstances.

In the Digital Millennium Copyright Act of 1998, Congress requested the U.S. Copyright Office of the Library of Congress to study the impact that copyright laws might have on online education. It recognized that changes in copyright law might be necessary to ensure that fair use of information is equally available to students and researchers in the digital as well as physical realm. Congress specifically directed that the law be reviewed "with an eye toward promoting distance education."

With input from publishers, higher education, libraries, and other users and producers, the Copyright Office presented its report, "Copyright and Digital Distance Education," to Congress in May 1999. The recommendations include clarifying the meaning of transmission to include digital as well as analog and eliminating the requirement of a physical classroom.

Copyright remains a major concern to educators, researchers, and librarians as well as publishers, developers, and copyright holders. Current copyright law governing distance education is over 20 years old and was based on broadcast models of telecourses for distance education. That law was not established with the virtual classroom in mind, nor does it resolve emerging issues of multimedia online, or provide a framework for permitting digital transmissions.

Educators and library representatives maintain that the current pay-per-view business model used in education bypasses, and thereby negates, explicit provisions in the copyright law intended to protect and encourage educational use of copyrighted material. They maintain that for web-based education to achieve its potential, students should be able to access remotely all educational material available to students in a physical classroom, and be able to do so from any location at any time.

Educational institutions seek the ability to use copyrighted works in a digital environment comparable to what the law currently allows in a face-to-face classroom. This current state of affairs is confusing and frustrating for educators. Many educational institutions report having difficulty with licensing for digital distance education. Professors complain about being forced to obtain licenses to use the same works in an online course that they are allowed to use under fair use provisions in a face-to-face classroom.

After teachers complete the task of determining who the copyright owner is, they often face delays in locating the owner, obtaining permission, and possibly incurring costs. The gap between the technology of distance learning and the language of the current copyright statute threatens the element of spontaneity from online instruction that the current statute affords in the analog world. It may cause online course developers to compromise their content, and has deterred some educators from entering the world of distance education altogether. These following examples were offered by the e-Testimony of the American Association of Community Colleges:

— A music instructor at Lake Land College in Mattoon, Illinois has the ability to play songs and other pieces of music in her classroom, but is faced with the prospect of drafting numerous letters seeking permission from copyright holders in order to incorporate these works into an online version of the same class.

— At Northwest Michigan College in Traverse City, Michigan, a children's literature instructor routinely displays many illustrations from children's books in her traditional class, but when considering an online version of the course must spend precious time and resources obtaining licenses for each of these works, or leave illustrations out of altogether.

— Current fair use exemptions allow a professor who comes across a work in the morning that perfectly illustrates a point to be made in that afternoon's lecture to use it for a traditional class. The same professor must wait until permission is granted to use it in an online version of the class. The confusion on digital copyright use can be especially frustrating for K-12 educators who want to demonstrate appropriate copyright use with their students but are limited in the time and resources they can devote to acquiring rights to materials.

Concern about inadvertent copyright infringement appears, in many school districts, to limit the effective use of the Internet as an educational tool. Schools are in a position of potential liability if a teacher or student fails to understand or appropriately apply copyright law and posts material on a school Web site. "The only way a school can fully protect against financial liability is to take a totally hands-off role with respect to the Web pages it posts on a school site, which no school should do."

Proposals to amend the Copyright Act and update fair use provisions are opposed by publishers. They correctly point out that the risks of unauthorized dissemination of copyrighted works are greater in an online environment than in a physical classroom, and maintain that technological safeguards are not yet widely available to prevent unauthorized uses. Without adequate safeguards the artists, writers, designers, programmers, and educators who create new works for instruction may not be appropriately compensated for their creativity.

The publishing industry is also concerned that the confusing landscape and consolidation of non-profits and for-profit providers of educational content make policy based on public versus private good difficult, if not impossible, to define.

Although the federal government has a legitimate role in monitoring how its funds are used and in protecting intellectual property, it is clear that a radical rethinking of the relevant body of regulation and law is in order. Otherwise the Internet will remain more a province of auctions and games, than a place for genuine learning. The virtual university is a reality. Unique in design but traditional in focus, virtual universities offer learners the opportunity to move beyond the barriers of physical space and time by taking courses online. The potential of the virtual university is seen in the offerings of companies like UNext. Founded in late 1997, UNext is committed to developing and delivering high-quality higher education to learners around the globe. It is this idea that led the company to launch Cardean University, an online university that delivers postsecondary business, executive, and professional education, and is authorized to offer a Master's degree in Business Administration. UNext and Cardean University have established a consortium of elite academic institutions including Columbia University, Stanford University, the University of Chicago, Carnegie Mellon University, and the London School of Economics and Political Science.

UNext is collaborating with faculty members from these institutions as well as other leading scholars and experts to produce a unique, state-of-the-art educational experience on the Internet. UNext focuses on "enhanced learning"-a learning platform that combines the advantages of a traditional university setting, such as community and collaboration, with the flexibility and responsiveness of online learning. Its approach is driven by one core idea: that the Internet fosters real learning because it facilitates collaborative and productive "learning by doing" activities. In this way, students, who may otherwise be unable to return for a graduate degree or who need continuing education, may enhance their skills and knowledge, and receive a chance at extending their learning prospects.

The Concord University School of Law provides another online model, one focusing on legal education. Because of work and family obligations, financial or geographic constraints, or even physical disability, many who want to become attorneys find that their goal is elusive. Founded in 1998 by Kaplan, Inc., Concord University School of Law provides legal education to people unable to attend a fixed facility program. On average, the Concord student is 40 years old. Nearly a third of students enrolled hold advanced degrees. Many Concord students live in communities where there is little or no access to a law school. Others have a law school in the area, but still choose Concord for the flexibility and convenience of its wholly online delivery.

Concord's curriculum, casebooks, and textbooks are the same as those found at law school campuses. Students access the curriculum through their "Personal Homepage," which provides an interactive syllabus for each course. Lectures are viewed on the Internet with students logging on at their convenience 24 hours a day, 7 days a week. Although Concord's virtual law school is only in its third year, the early reports show good results. The initial groups of Concord students sitting for the First Year Law Student Examination in California had first-time pass rates ranging from 20 percent to 33 percent higher than the state average. They scored 80 percent higher than students from other American Bar Association-approved programs who have been required to take the exam during the last five years.

A third approach is OnlineLearning.net, one of the largest virtual universities in the U.S. OnlineLearning.net selects prominent university partners and then helps them produce and market their fully accredited courses and programs to working professionals. The classes are small in size, interactive, instructor-led, and highly collaborative. In addition, it provides students with an "online concierge" in every course, and has a unique online faculty and instructor development program. More than 90 percent of the students enrolled in courses complete them, with 85 percent rating the courses "as good or better than face-to-face learning."

The University of Phoenix Online program was started in 1989 and has been providing complete degree programs for working adult students for over a decade. With 1,200 faculty members, it currently offers 10 accredited degree programs in business, education, information technology, and nursing. Currently over 15,000 students attend class via the online program. While the University's enrollments have grown at over 22 percent per year, the Online campus has routinely grown at over 50 percent per year. The popularity of this program is proof that there is a demand for alternative delivery modes in higher education.

Virtual universities are helping learners connect with a new world of educational opportunities. Through these and similar programs students around the world are accessing the best educational resources-anytime, anywhere, at any stage in life.

Privacy and Protection

The Internet carries with it danger as well as promise. Advertising can interfere with the learning process and take advantage of a captive audience of learners- of all types and ages. Privacy can be endangered when data is collected on users of online materials. Students, especially young children, need protections from harmful or inappropriate intrusions in their learning environments.

While many consider materials on the Web to be free, "banner ads" and other forms of online advertising support much of the material. Some maintain that schools should consider this as a non-intrusive tradeoff for high quality online content. They argue that commercialism is a part of society, has been a part of the school environment for years, and that students largely ignore product advertisements.

Critics decry the extension of advertisers into the school, and their added power in the online environment. They counter that, if students are expected to ignore ads, then why are companies spending millions to "capture the eyeballs" of the youth market? Advertisers are "You'll look up and down streets. Look 'em over with care. About some you will say, 'I don't choose to go there.' With your head full of brains and your shoes full of feet, You're too smart to go down any not-so-good streets."

Some companies have gone further by providing whole systems to schools, including computer labs, online access, and software, in return for advertising that appears when the Internet is accessed from these facilities. The ZapMe Netspace was one such effort. It offered a 2 x 4 inch banner ad window that presented multimedia ads to students at all times, with the ads changing every 15 seconds, exposing students to approximately 200 ads in a 50- minute class period. Some schools and districts have gone the opposite direction, banning advertising altogether. In 1998, the National Association of State Boards of Education of US developed a set of principles to guide state boards in the development of policy regarding corporate involvement in schools. Among the principles for "positive school-business relationships" were the following:

— Corporate involvement shall not require students to observe, listen to, or read commercial advertising.

— Selling or providing access to a captive audience in the classroom for commercial purposes is exploitation and a violation of public trust.

Online Profiling:Online profiling is the collection of information from and about an individual as he or she uses the Internet. This can be accomplished either through the collection of personal data a user provides or through the use of screen name or identifier "cookies" placed on a hard drive by the Web site or third-party delivering ads to a Web site.

Many consumers are unaware when they are being profiled or that profiling is in fact a sophisticated form of personalized marketing. A recent Business-Week/ Harris Poll found that only 40 percent of those surveyed had even heard of cookies, and only 75 percent of those who had knew what they were. This lack of understanding is a special concern for students and young children, unsophisticated as they are in the importance of protecting information privacy. Children, and even teenagers, may not have yet developed the sophisticated skills to understand why they should not provide information to others online.

A recent study by the Annenberg Public Policy Center found that, although young people expressed concerns about protecting privacy and information that may be collected about them on Web sites, when offered a free gift in exchange for personal or family information, many more children than parents were willing to provide this information. Young People and the "Dark Streets" A more direct threat is children's exposure to violence, pornography, and predators on the Web.

In US, a recent study entitled *Online Victimization: A Report on the Nation's Youth,* conducted interviews with a nationally representative sample of 1,500 youths ages 10-17 who use the Internet. The study found that large numbers of youths are encountering offensive experiences on the Internet. Twenty percent were sexually solicited. Six percent were harassed. The offenses and offenders are diverse, not just men trolling for sex. Much of the offending behavior comes from other youth, and some from women.

Teenagers are the primary targets, creating a different sort of challenge than would be the case if younger children, over whom parents have more control, were the primary targets. Although most solicitations fail, the sheer numbers are alarming. Several million young people, ages 10 to 17, are sexually propositioned on the Internet every year. Furthermore, sexual material is intrusive on the Internet. One in 4 youths surveyed had an unwanted exposure to pictures that included nudity or even more graphic sexual scenes.

Although all these offenses are troubling, most youths do not tell parents, teachers, or even their friends about them. Even when parents are aware of the offenses, they, like their children, do not know where to report them. The authors of the study emphasize that Internet friendships between teens and adults are not uncommon and are generally benign. In fact, the opportunity for people of all ages to congregate and chat online about common interests is one of the great strengths of the Internet, and one of the reasons it can be so useful for young people as they reach out to individuals who can be positive role models and mentors.

The Internet is far from the only, or the greatest, threat to young people in the society. Among respondents in the study, 30 percent had been attacked in real life by other youths in the last year. Other studies on school violence make it clear that child victimization in the online world is dwarfed by what they experience in the real world.

Protection comes in many forms and levels of control ranging from legislation to voluntary acceptable-use policies, to technical solutions like filters, monitoring systems, and portals, to consumer empowerment systems like ratings and consumer and learner education. No one "solution" is perfect-each has benefits, each has limitations. Their potential utility depends on personal and community preferences as well as the setting.

The Children's Online Privacy Protection Act (COPPA) went into effect April 2000. It regulates the collection of personal information from children under the age of 13. It requires commercial Web sites targeted at children under 13 to secure parental permission before collecting, using, or disclosing personal information from children. These sites must also post a privacy policy detailing what personal information is being collected, how it is to be used, and if it will be given to third parties. While most witnesses who testified before the Commission support the underlying intent of COPPA, several concerns were raised:

— COPPA does not cover teens, an especially vulnerable group for online victimization as noted above. Teens are also major targets for online profiling and marketing.

— Current "opt-in" requirements for "verifiable parental consent" may unduly restrict children's access to valuable online educational resources in schools.

— COPPA's administrative and record-keeping burdens for schools are substantial and may be enough to discourage full usage of the Internet. The US School Boards Association and American Association of School Administrators predict "the drastic increase of schools' administrative responsibilities prior to engaging their students in online activity would have a 'chilling' effect on the positive, productive collaborations of educational businesses and schools."

Of equal concern is the dampening effect COPPA requirements could have on innovative uses of the Internet for delivering personalized content and assessment materials. The regular collection of student data is necessary for these systems to function. One proposal suggested throughout the Commission's hearings would allow parents of young children to "opt-out" of their child's participation in an online activity or service. Filtering or blocking software is an approach advocated by many.

Legislation has been proposed that would prevent schools from receiving E-rate funding for discounted Internet use unless they filter Web content. Witnesses voiced concern with this approach for both practical and philosophical reasons. On the practical side, filters are not foolproof. Often unwanted material gets through.Other times valid content may be screened out inappropriately. One-third of the families surveyed in the online victimization study report that they currently use filters. However, 5 percent say they have stopped using them, suggesting some level of dissatisfaction. There is also the philosophical concern about filters in public institutions like libraries, raising freedom of information issues. One witness suggested that purveyors of objectionable material could be required to check a database of those who opt out of receiving this material. Those who receive objectionable material online against their stated wishes could then have legal recourse.

Monitoring systems are software solutions that provide a record of the sites a person has visited on the Internet. Most browsers keep at least a short-term record, and more complex monitoring systems can collect past visits by viewer. This is a relatively simple, low-cost solution for parents and schools, who can link accountability with education efforts and attach consequences for inappropriate or unauthorized activity.

Approximately three-fifths of households surveyed in the online victimization study reported that parents or guardians checked the computer history function to see where their children had been travelling on the Internet.

Obviously, monitoring systems are only as good as the amount of attention they are given by those supervising students' Internet use.

Ratings systems put the power of choice back on the user, school, parent, or other authority figure supervising students' use of the Internet. Like ratings for movies, television, software, and now video games and music, the rationale is to give the consumer a choice. The Internet Content Rating Association (ICRA) is an independent, nonprofit organization that promotes protecting the student on internet.

Monitoring Systems: Monitoring systems keep a record of which sites have been accessed, how much time is spent on them, and to whom e-mail messages have been sent. Limits the amount of time students are online, or the specific times of day it is possible to go online. Search engines designed to locate only information approved for children.

Recreational Software Advisory Council on the Internet, managed by the Internet Content Rating Association, provides consumers information about the level of sex, nudity, violence, and offensive language in Web sites.

Although they differ in form, all filters allow access to a restricted collection of Web sites. Access may be either provided to approved sites or blocked to sites that are considered off-limits.

Contracts signed by students and parents setting guidelines for use of the Internet. Schools, libraries, and community centers often create their own policies based on their local contexts.

The value of ICRA ratings has been debated, especially as the self-assessment aspect of the system may not correspond with judgments a parent or teacher might make regarding the level of intensity of questionable content. Furthermore, as Web sites change rapidly, keeping a rating system up to date is nearly impossible. Portals offer a gateway to pre-selected, screened sites around a particular area of interest. They often combine the features of a firewall and a ratings system by assuring that offensive materials or those inappropriate for children will not be included. Portals provide a way for parents and educators to guide students not only to sites that have been deemed of value, but also to those that do not present negative online experiences. Acceptable use policies and education are solutions supported by all witnesses before the Commission. Educators, parents, and those who work with young people need to be aware of the dangers the Internet can pose to the privacy and safety of all users. Families need to know about various strategies and tools they can use to guide and protect themselves.

Communities-including schools and libraries-must develop standards for what they consider appropriate monitoring of Internet usage for various age groups. These communities of users, from community to classroom to family, must develop and abide by acceptable use policies they feel comfortable with, along with appropriate sanctions for irresponsible behavior. Educators and parents must teach young people what it means to be safe and responsible online citizens. Learning that there are dark streets on the Web and in real life is a necessary lesson in the education of today's modern student. Regrettable as is it may be, this lesson is an integral part of becoming a learner in today's society.

In some ways, school Internet capital expenses are equivalent to the expenditures a district makes in purchasing a fleet of school buses. After the initial cost of the purchase, the school buses require fuel, maintenance, trained drivers, parking lots to house them, insurance, and upgrades to keep the fleet current. It is the same with technology.

The continuing operational costs of maintaining and using the technology dwarf initial purchase and installation costs. These costs include: payments to utility and Internet service providers; technical support; instructional content; renovations to the physical plant; trained educators and administrators; and upgrades as newer equipment comes on line.

Too often educational institutions have focused on startup costs without planning for the substantial and continuing costs of operation. When this occurs, technology, like unused buses, is relegated to the "garage" and has little value to anyone. Schools and colleges are beginning to adopt "total cost of ownership" (TCO) models that have been used for years by the business community.

This approach breaks down into component parts each of the expenses involved in using technology so they can be more clearly analyzed. For example, Quality Education Data (QED) reports that K-12 schools spent an average of $122 per student on technology support during the 1998-99 school year.

A 1998 survey 3 of 29 large urban school districts found that technology budgets ranged from $22 per student to $584 per student. The average hovered in the $120 to $130 range per student. Most financing models indicate that the initial costs of hardware purchases and installation, along with retrofitting of old buildings to support an upgraded infrastructure, represent the bulk of costs when amortized over five years. It is assumed that costs then shift to non-capital, or operating expenses. But in reality, K-12 technology expenditures skew heavily on the side of hardware.

A survey of 400 district and school level officials found that schools were spending 55 percent of total costs on hardware, 16 percent on networking, 9 percent on software, and only 6 percent on training, with another 6 percent on service and support, 5 percent on supplies, and 1 percent on online services. What seems clear is that schools are under-investing in the personnel and support needed to make their technology investments most useful. In some ways this is a result of the way technology is funded in schools and colleges.

Technology startup costs have often been funded with capital dollars raised by bond issues and special grants that may be easier to raise than the continuing operating funds required for ongoing costs. Yet it is these continuing service and personnel costs that are often most critical to technology integration in an educational environment.

Fudning

Education for America's elementary and secondary schools is primarily the responsibility of states and localities. The funding follows this pattern. States provide approximately 44 percent and localities close to 40 percent of the US's expenditures for elementary and secondary education, while foundations, in-kind activities and others sources provide 10.2 percent of funding. The federal government currently contributes only 6.1 percent of all elementary and secondary education funds.

The federal share of education funding overall has declined, from 13.9 percent in fiscal 1980 to 6.1 percent in fiscal 1998. This declining federal funding share is also true for higher education, where the federal share was 18 percent in fiscal 1980 and dropped to 12.1 percent in fiscal 1998.

Nonetheless, there are areas where federal dollars have a major impact. The federal government has made a large-scale investment in the future through its support of technology at the K-12 level. Estimates place the current federal share of education technology investment at about $1.5 billion, or between 20 percent 7 and 35 percent 8 of all elementary and secondary technology outlays.

The $1.5 billion federal funding for education technology comes from both targeted programs for technology as well as via core or "traditional" federal programs. In the former category of direct education technology programs are the Technology Literacy Challenge Fund funded at $425 million in fiscal 2000 as well as the Technology Innovation Challenge Grant program for stimulating technology-supported high performance learning environments, funded at $146 million in fiscal 2000. Other specialized technology programs include:

— Preparing Tomorrow's Teachers to Use Technology (PT3)-funded at $75 million in fiscal 2000

— Community-based Technology Programs—$32.5 million

— Stars School Program: $50.5 million

— Learning Anytime, Anywhere Partnerships: $23.3 million

— Technology and Media Services: $36 million

— Assistive Technology for the disabled learner: $34 million

An even greater portion of federal education technology funding support comes through core federal programs which have made school hardware and software acquisition, as well as staff development for technology, a greater priority in recent years. These include:

— Title I grants for basic and advanced skills-Approximately $500 million of this $8 billion annual program is used by schools to support technology investment. Title I provides almost a third of all software and hardware used in basic skills instruction in schools.

— Title VI Innovative Education Strategies-Approximately $125 million to $150 million a year is spent on upgrading technology in schools.

— Title II Eisenhower Professional Development-With total funding in fiscal 2000 of $335 million, this program places a priority on teacher training with technology, and allows low-income schools to use all Eisenhower funds for hardware and software purchases.

— Goals 2000 Educate America Act-Fiscal 2000 funding is $491 million. A large portion of these funds is spent by states and school districts on technology planning.

— Vocational and Adult Education-School districts use approximately $250 million for technological capacity building. In addition to the federal investment in education technology, states and school districts contribute another $5.4 billion for instructional technology via a myriad of district-wide programs and competitive grants.

— Telecommunications Funding: Intersecting State and Federal Responsibility Missing from these amounts, however, is funding for telecommunications access made possible through the E-rate program.

Enacted as a part of the Universal Service Program of the Telecommunications Act of 1996, the E-rate program provides discounts to public and private schools, libraries, and consortia on the costs of telecommunications services, internal access, and internal networking. In the program's first two years, tens of thousands of public and private elementary and secondary schools, and thousands more libraries received a total of $3.66 billion in discounts on connectivity and telecommunications services.

In the Spring of 2000, the Federal Communications Commission announced that the third year of the program would be funded at $2.25 billion, the maximum allowed, based on requests submitted by schools and libraries around US.

Telecommunications and education policy present an intersection of state and federal responsibility. The federal telecommunications funding mechanism that provides universal service offers a basic level of service to individuals regardless of where they live. This subsidy is in effect an "equal opportunity access guarantee" that applies equally to individuals wherever they live.

The E-rate sits at the intersection of this juncture, as it was developed on the belief that the Internet should provide a place where all learners can find information and opportunities for anytime, anyplace learning. The funding subsidy it provides is leveling the Internet playing field for education.

In this new environment, two things are clear: funding must be sustained, and new approaches must be considered. Old models do not meet new realities. It makes little sense to use 30-year bonds to purchase equipment that should be replaced in 3 years. Schools should examine how technology costs in one area can be offset by efficiencies in other areas.

The productivity gains found in business through investments in technology took 3 decades to emerge. Today these investments are considered a foundation of the U.S. economy, accounting for a third of its growth. Similar growth in educational productivity might be derived through technology, but only if other changes are adopted that support more productive educational environments.

Streamlining administrative procedures is an obvious example. Web-based test administration could bring significant cost savings in assessment expenditures. Likewise, savings in textbook and instructional materials budgets may be achieved if the licensing, distribution, and updating of these are made less expensive online. Teacher training online may be a more efficient use of time and resources than paying for substitutes when teachers are pulled away from their classrooms.

But if technology is used as an add-on to existing activities, rather than as a means to reshape education, then it will simply add to the total cost of operations and few savings will be realized. Business has learned that productivity gains and cost savings come only when old ways of doing business are abandoned and technological solutions replace them. For example, when universities can reach students through online courses, they can reevaluate their budgets for building more "bricks and mortar" campuses.

There is nothing magical about traditional classroom practice. Educationally, students require a mix of pedagogical support, guidance, and supervision, which can be provided in a myriad of ways. The U.S. classroom is a 150 year-old, relatively low-cost technology, worn out by time and changed conditions for meeting these requirements.

Perhaps the much sought after Internet "killer" application for education is not an application at all, but the potential for reorganizing education and for connecting communities of students, teachers, parents, and highly qualified volunteer experts.

Investing in the development and support of skilled teachers, and supplementing the expertise of a given teacher with the distributed expertise of the broader education community, offers great promise. The possibility of making "the best and the brightest" of the teaching profession available to learners in places where accidents of geography and economics have led to lower quality educational experiences suggests that the Internet can impact the economics of education in ways we have only just begun to imagine.

A number of witnesses offered a range of funding model proposals that might address the continuing technology requirements of the education sector. These suggestions fall into the following categories:

— Tax incentives to encourage educational investments in areas of high cost and high need

— User taxes on corporate technology purchases

— Public and private partnerships in building and renovating schools to provide high tech centers an entire community can use during non-school hours, supported through user fees

— Increased federal and state appropriations for technology and web-based learning opportunities

— A learning technology trust fund that could combine these models to help sustain long-term school technology investment momentum

Business should play a much larger role in helping schools make technology support their educational needs. All businesses-not just high tech companies-have a substantial stake in this area. Banks and retailers, food and beverage companies, and clothing manufacturers all need employees with greater technical capabilities than the schools are currently providing to fill the high-skilled jobs necessary in today's economy. Isolated donations of hardware or software, while potentially helpful, are simply not enough.

Content, equipment, and services costs associated with web-based technologies can be brought down in several ways. Aggregated purchasing would enable suppliers to lower their per unit prices. Many states already purchase technology by aggregating demand, and some state and district education systems are joining in. But more could be done to capture potential economies of scale throughout the education sector.

The development of standardized education technology packages helps build significant volume to purchases. By making these packages modular and scalable, schools could select appropriate technology and network components at the lowest cost and most effective price point. Other costs include time spent in planning, installing, managing, and upgrading systems. Some institutions have found that hardware, software, and services integrated into packages suitable for different needs and circumstances takes much of the complexity out of planning multimedia network computing installations. Remote management of local school networks can ultimately remove the need for expensive onsite technical personnel, as well as provide higher quality service.

The use of existing internationally recognized standards such as Internet protocols, and the development of additional standards, have the potential of creating packages with enormous market demand, attracting suppliers to the education market, and promoting competition in price and capabilities. This type of standardization, quite common in other areas served by technology, could help lower prices and improve performance in education as well.

The development of an efficient network architecture can also help build economies of scale. Designing multi-user/use platforms means that more value can be obtained from hardware and service configurations. Careful network and communications backbone architecture is critical to lowering communications costs. The backbone architecture issues go beyond the design and management capabilities of any school district, but collaborations could be as cost-effective for education as such networks are in other areas. State networks that are in place and ready to link to the Internet2 backbone could offer the most technology access for the dollar.

In many cases, the use of networked computing will enable schools to significantly revamp and modernize their educational programs. Opportunities to expand individualized learning, provide access to a much broader and richer set of educational materials and human resources, and promote "learning-to-learn" skills will often require changes in how the educational institutions are organized and funded. If schools and universities are to be held accountable for improving educational outcomes based on the investments made using technology, they will need help from government, business, and public sector partners at all levels.

The Web-based Commission believes a national mobilization is necessary, one that evokes a response similar in scope to other great American opportunities-or crises: Sputnik and the race to the moon, bringing electricity and phone service to all corners of the nation, finding a vaccine for polio.

The very idea of the World Wide Web is one of connections. The ability to use the Internet to reshape learning requires actions that are also interrelated and interconnected.

The Commission saw first-hand the policies that most influence technology use in education derive from bottom-up, interconnected grassroots efforts far more than from top-down dictates. The nation needs to tap into this energy and use it to shape education policy for the Internet age.

The idea of connectedness also applies to the reality of the current learning environment. The core barriers to effective Internet use identified by the Commission cannot be addressed in isolation. They are inextricably linked. As such, they pose an even greater challenge that can be resolved only through a widespread mobilization effort. That effort, therefore, must work to assure:

— Universal broadband access at home, at school, and at work in support of learner-centered, anytime, anywhere, any pace educational opportunity

— High quality, on-demand, and continuous professional development and support for educators and administrators at all levels

— A new education research agenda that is well-funded and focused on how people learn in the Internet age

— Online educational content that is widely available, affordable, and meets the highest standards of educational excellence

— Relief from regulatory and administrative requirements that do not accommodate innovations in learning

— Reliable safeguards to protect online learners and ensure their privacy

— Sustained funding-via traditional and new sources-that meets the challenge of learning transformation

National Call to Action

The US congressional Web-based Education Commission calls on the new Congress and Administration to embrace an "e-learning" agenda as a centerpiece of US's federal education policy. This e-learning agenda should be aimed at assisting local communities, state eduction agencies, institutions of higher education, and the private sector to maximize the power of the Internet for learning. In the next two years, the 107th Congress and new

Administration are required to revise the major laws guiding federal involvement in K-12 education. The reauthorization of the Elementary and Secondary Education Act will, in large part, determine federal education priorities and the tens of billions of spending that go with them for the next five years.

Congress and the Administration will also consider new funding authority for education research. They are likely to revisit the issues of safeguarding children online, copyright law in the digital age, advertising in education, and other "rules of the road" issues related to the Internet. Finally, Congress and the Administration will begin preparations for revising the student financial assistance laws as part of the reauthorization of the Higher Education Act.

The opportunity has never been better for establishing meaningful public policy aimed at maximizing the power of the Internet for learning as a fundamental element of education at all levels. The commission urge the Congress and President to seize this opportunity and to focus on ways in which these public laws can be modified and changed to support, rather than undermine, the technology that is so dramatically changing education.

The commission call on federal and state governments to make the extension of broadband access for all learners a central goal of telecommunications policy. The commission urge federal and state policymakers to adopt a policy framework that will help accelerate broadband deployment in education quickly and effectively. The E-rate program, which has brought 21st Century telecommunications into the US schools and libraries, has provided a dramatic boost. Individual state efforts have shown promise and success. Policymakers in state and local jurisdictions should consider complementary efforts focused on educational applications of broadband access.

Federal and state policymakers should also consider legislative changes designed to achieve speedy deployment of broadband technologies at educational institutions, particularly for those communities of learners on the other side of the "Digital Divide." Better collection of data on current access levels, costs, and availability of broadband services will facilitate this goal.

Greater Internet access for education enables the private sector to build the base of skilled workers it needs to operate in the global economy and to expand its market for enhanced telecommunications goods and services. This opportunity brings with it responsibilities for helping to build and support this capacity. Policymakers should seek out new partnership opportunities focused on high quality services, affordable rates, and sustained upgrades and improvement in access.

The commission call on policymakers at all levels to work with educational institutions and the private sector to support the continuous growth of educators through the use of technology.

Educators are the ultimate knowledge workers. The commission knows that more and different training will be necessary if teachers, administrators, and faculty members are to integrate the advances of technology into the curriculum and into their teaching. To do so will require a major new direction and commitment from policymakers, from the private sector, and from educators themselves.

Congress has begun to focus on building the institutional capacity to assure that the next generation of teachers uses technology as effortlessly and effectively as workers in other industries. The commission encourage continuing support for these efforts, along with initiatives and models that make just-in-time, just-what's-needed training and support available to educators.

The reauthorization of the Elementary and Secondary Education Act offers the opportunity to make this happen and to incorporate the best thinking and practices identified by this Commission. In addition, the Higher Education Act reauthorization down the line will provide another vehicle to articulate the federal role in professional development.

Partnerships that bring together the federal government, state and local agencies, the private sector, and educational institutions offer the promise of assuring continuing teacher empowerment and growth with technology. Federal funding through such important efforts as the Preparing

Tomorrow's Teachers for Technology program primes the pump for these collaborations. States can share in the development and distribution of e-learning courses, programs, and materials for teacher education and professional development. They can also work together to adopt common frameworks for building the competencies and performance assessments of new teacher expertise and build policies that allow for cross-state teacher certification.

The universities, and the colleges of education within them, should make the development of highly skilled 21st Century educators their most important priority; and they should fund and support teacher and administrator preparation programs accordingly.

The commission call upon the Federal government to create a comprehensive research, development, and innovation framework for learning technology.

A commission appointed in 1997 by US President Bill Clinton called for a rigorous empirical research program at a level equal to at least 0.5 percent of the aggregate spending on K-12 education. This has not happened and with the passage of time the urgency of this goal is even more critical.

To achieve this goal, the Commission recommends:

— Establishing a benchmark goal for federal R & D investment in web-based learning, consistent with similar benchmarks in other industry segments. A possible approach could be the creation of a "Synergy Superfund," a continuous funding source to advance necessary public-private partnerships to build the fast turn-around of technological breakthroughs with applications for learning.

— Focusing on high payback targets of educational opportunity where present links between learning theory and technological innovation appear particularly promising. These include such areas as new forms of assessment of learning, early reading content, and the conceptual stumbling blocks that impact understanding and achievement in mathematics and the sciences.

— Supporting the creation of learning communities and tools for collaborative knowledge building and dissemination among researchers, teachers, and developers. Funding and regulatory support for public-private partnerships, and cross-institution and cross-agency collaboration in R & D could make it possible to bring promising ideas to practice quickly and efficiently by using the Internet as a research and dissemination tool.

— Supporting a sustained effort to track the use of the Internet in education and how the Web is transforming learning. A particular focus should be on the effectiveness of the policy actions implemented to address the key barriers to web-based education.

The commission call upon the public and private sectors to join forces in developing high quality content and applications for online learning. There is an increasing body of good content for e-learning, but it presents only a small glimmer of what is possible. And it is difficult for the consumer to sort the wheat from the chaff, to make sense of all the "clutter" on the Web. Compounding this problem is a risky private capital market for development, particularly at the preK-12 level.

At the federal level, the Commission recommends that:

— Congress articulate content development priorities and seed funding for development of web-based content and applications in high need areas. It should also encourage collaboration and partnerships between the public and private sectors in the development and distribution of high quality online courses, learning tools, and materials.

— Federal agencies and programs should adopt technical standards for the design of online courses and the meta-tagging of digital content. These should include universal design standards for access for those with disabilities.

For the education community, the Commission recommends:

— Continuing the current voluntary system of accrediting higher education institutions and programs. However, the range of programs and new providers suggests the need for better clarity for the consumer regarding what accreditation means. The joint development of a "consumer's guide to accreditation" by the federal government and the higher education community would be an important contribution.

— Creating mechanisms for users to share their commercial and noncommercial resources and experiences regarding online courses and programs. Experimentation with online user reviews for content similar to that found on commercial sites could empower the informed choice of educators.

— Articulating frameworks for what constitutes good online courses and encouraging private sector education providers to develop their courseware in concert with these frameworks.

For the states, the Commission recommends convening state and regional education accreditors and organizations to build common frameworks and requirements for online learning programs, courses, and certifications comparable to those required for onsite programs.

The commission call on Congress, the U.S. Department of Education, and state and regional education funding and regulatory authorities to remove barriers that block full learner access to online learning resources, courses, and programs while ensuring accountability of taxpayer dollars. Witnesses spoke forcefully and effectively about how federal, state, and local education regulations written for an earlier education system no longer work in today's borderless, timeless "anywhere, anyplace" learning environment. There are some areas where federal action may be appropriate.

The Commission recommends a full review and, if necessary, a revision of the 12-hour rule, 50 percent rule, and incentive compensation requirements that are creating barriers to students enrolling in online and distance education courses. The commission call on the Department of Education, Congress, the higher education community, and the private sector to continue to work together in devising alternatives for measuring student financial assistance eligibility to accommodate online learning opportunity.

The Commission also encourages states to:

— Work with organizations such as the National Governors' Association, the National Conference of State Legislatures, the Education Commission of the States, the Council of Chief State School Officers, the State Higher Education Executive Officers, and the National Association of State Boards of Education to convene and provide incentives for collaboration among educators, content providers, and regulators that span state or regional boundaries.

— Recognize and support efforts to increase cross-state regulatory and administrative cooperation modeled after the Southern Regional Education Board and the Western Interstate Cooperative in Higher Education. Such efforts should be encouraged to develop policies that address the transfer and awarding of academic credit earned online; faculty workload, compensation, and online content ownership issues; financing of distance learning; quality assurance in distance learning; online student services; and programs that reach underrepresented student populations.

The Commission endorses the U.S. Copyright Office proposal to convene education representatives and publisher stakeholders in order to build greater consensus and understanding of the "fair use" doctrine and its application in web-based education. The goal should be agreement on guidelines for the appropriate digital uses of information and consensus on the licensing of content not covered by the fair use doctrine.

The Commission believes that filtering and blocking software alone is of limited value in this regard. Instead, the Commission recommends:

— Encouraging developers and educators to collaborate in creating noncommercial, high quality educational zones that could be easily accessed by educators, parents, and children.

— Promoting efforts involving states, districts, and schools that will result in education programs that empower students to use the Internet safely, wisely and ethically.

Educational programs should be built around appropriate use policies that set clearly understood and locally derived standards. These programs should reach out beyond students and include parents, teachers, and administrators.

The Commission believes that the Children's Online Privacy and Protection Act (COPPA) provides important protections for young children. Nevertheless, all students, especially teenagers not covered by COPPA, need to understand threats to privacy and the implications of inappropriate disclosure of information. The education market should speak with one voice in demanding that young people and their families have access to information already collected and the opportunity to correct, prevent, or curtail the use of their personal information.

If the Web is to be used to its fullest powers for personalized, interactive learning, the collection of some identifiable student information online may be necessary. Parental permission may be better directed as an "opt-out" rather than "opt-in" requirement for student participation in online learning activities. This suggests that some adjustments to COPPA may be necessary to allow educational exemptions from current verifiable parental consent requirements.

The Commission encourages local and state education agencies to aggregate their market strength in order to bring advanced broadband technologies to preK-12, postsecondary, and adult education at considerably lower costs. The commission also believe that states can encourage deployment of broadband access through their support of similar tax incentives and targeting of funding in high-need areas. In addition, states have a special opportunity to create and fund networks that can be linked to the Internet2 backbone and bring state-of-the-art technology applications to educational institutions.

CHAPTER 3

Participation in Education

The persistence of poverty in many parts of the world after decades of so-called 'development' and the sea changes occurring more generally today in political, social, and cultural life have once again made education an issue of critical importance. The transformation of the macro-political landscape, the promise of expanded democratization, the threat of narrow nationalism and fundamentalism, the increasing risks of environmental degradation and endemic disease - all of these challenges call for the more effective development of human resources and thus for a greater demand for, and supply of, education of better quality.

But just as so much hope is being placed on education, doubts about the general vision of education systems, the actual availability of schooling, and the quality of education of education have increased. In much of the world, especially the least developed, education is becoming less, rather than more, available. In many countries, the growth of primary school enrolments is declining while the absolute numbers of illiterate adults and of school-age children not in school are increasing.

Even in countries where enrolment rates have continued to grow, a sizeable percentage of children and adults often remains unreached by primary schooling and literacy programmes. These trends, which particularly affect education for girls and women, reflect two things:

(1) declining individual demand for an education seen as being irrelevant to a family's current welfare and a student's future success, and

(2) declining public investment in education measured both as a percentage of the national budget and as per pupil expenditures.

The disturbing trends are not only quantitative in nature. In many countries, both research data and more anecdotal observation indicate an erosion in the general quality of education provided to learners as defined in traditional terms of inputs (teachers, facilities, books, and supplies), outputs (literacy and completion rates, achievement scores), and processes (the nature of the teaching-learning act).

A final, and perhaps most important doubt, concerns the narrowness of the traditional vision of what 'good' education is and what it is meant to achieve. It can be argued today that good education, given the state of the world described above, must now be defined not only in relation to the extent to which a school is well-housed and well-supplied; teaches literacy, job skills, and 'facts for life' and facilitates an effective teaching-learning process. Education of good quality must also, by definition:

— encourage a more integrated view of how the world operates and how development does (or does not) occur,

— make students more critically aware of how their actions, individually and collectively, will hinder or help the world to meet future challenges; and

— help to mobilize and empower people with the knowledge and skills to participate more actively, more democratically, and more collectively in the development process.

The problem is that in order to achieve such a vision, while at the same time increasing the availability and the quality of education more traditionally defined, most education systems of the world would need to be considerably reformed.

Given the history of educational reform, however, it is not easy to be optimistic about the possibility of altering a given system in significant ways. Such history shows that in the past, many (if not most) traditional, large-scale reforms designed by central governments - both conventional reforms and alternative, more non-formal innovations - have proven very difficult to implement, disseminate, and sustain. Debt and recession, the isolation of marginal populations, and the interruptions of war and natural disaster share much of the blame for this persistent inability of many governments both to supply an increasing (or even a constant) number of educational places and to improve, on a day-to-day basis, the quality of education occurring in their schools - let alone redefine the very nature of education itself.

But the character of centralized bureaucracies and of their technocratic planning techniques also play an important role in this regard. Thus, the traditional community-based education model found in many societies, where communities "provided new generations of young people with the education necessary for transmitting local norms and economic skills...[and where] education was deeply embedded in local social relations [and]...government played a minor role", gave way to a more standardized, uniform, and centralized government-provided model. In this model education - often with unfortunate results -" came to be viewed as appropriate and necessary for everyone and as such was the proper business of government...through formal school systems, coordinated by bureaucracies placed above the community". The limitations of this model have now become clear. They arise from the fact that:

— governments often lack funds to provide all communities with the necessary education and thus are often unable to guarantee a sufficient education to all children;

— the management capacity of bureaucracies has not kept up with the expansion of the system and the sheer magnitude and complexity of the problems; and

— "centrally-designed programmes are seldom responsive to the needs of the poor, and the organizations through which they are implemented seldom have the capacity to implement these projects as designed, let alone identify the actual needs and adapt the project accordingly".

In the words of a manager of a 'basic school' in Mali:

> "The State can not descend to the level of the school. Even if it is able to do so, it does it with a level of information so inadequate that its intervention is completely inefficacious. The multiplicity of structures which form a screen between the central level and the level of the school alters all information.... Moreover, the central level is too 'specialized' and imagines itself on a pedestal too high to 'descend' and to 'lower itself' to the level of the classroom".

Despite such limitations, and in the face of the economic, social, political, and educational issues discussed above, planners and managers have no choice but to make further attempts to reorganize and reform education systems and processes. In doing so, they face several challenges.

— They need to respond more effectively to a much broader context of development. Problems such as poverty, environmental degradation, and the spread of HIV/AIDS need to intrude much more sharply into the consciousness and everyday work of planners and managers. Education systems need to discuss such problems more frankly, deliver messages about them more effectively, and respond more immediately and forcefully to their impact.

— Planners and managers need to concern themselves with issues larger than the nature of inputs and outputs in narrowly focused, formal education systems. They need to understand better the links between schooling and its social and cultural environment, the kind of socialization and informal learning provided to children both before school entry and outside of the classroom, and ways to develop more literate and supportive environments in the family and the community surrounding the school. Thus, for example, they need to work more closely with the more non-formal, frequently more innovative (and non-governmental) education programmes often available to mothers, out-of-school youth, and adult learners.

— In order to reach those marginal populations often most in need of greater involvement in development programmes, planners and managers must create educational systems and processes more flexible and non-formal in nature. These will likely be characterized by school calendars and class timetables, entry ages, curricula, and teaching methods quite different from those found in traditional age- and grade-bound schools and classrooms.

— Planners and managers need to understand the importance of broad partnerships in development and to see their task not merely to improve the efficiency and effectiveness of their own sector's delivery system, narrowly defined, but also to assist and collaborate with other sectors (health, community services, agriculture) and other actors (NGOs, community associations, local government, universities) in encouraging a more participatory development process. Such a process - unlike the traditional technocratic, top-down approach - can increase the control of people over development processes; lead to more resources from a wider range of actors; increase programme demand, relevance, efficiency, and sustainability; and develop new knowledge, skills, and attitudes in those participating in the process.

But bringing planners and managers to such an understanding is not an easy thing to do. It requires the development of a set of institutional norms and policies which promote more participatory approaches to development. These relate to:

1. the 'openness' of schools, education systems, and bureaucracies:
   — to more non-traditional, non-formal approaches to education; to the gaze, support, and appropriate intervention of other partners;
   — to new ideas, especially from lower levels of the system, and to new ways of doing things; and
   — to change, and to the flexibility and adaptability such change requires.
2. collaboration and participation across and among various actors in eduction, both inside and outside of the sector (other development sectors, local government, parents, community organizations, NGOs, private enterprise), so that:
   — these actors share responsibility for education and feel common ownership of the education system and common accountability for its quality;
   — such participation, by definition, becomes an accepted characteristic of 'good' education, and
   — government planners and managers become aware of the power of a new '-collaborative' model of education which recognizes both government and the community as important actors in improving the quality and relevance of basic education broadly defined.

3. the need for the system itself to become more participatory in nature - in needs assessment, goal setting, research, planning, management, Participation for educational change:

   — a synthesis of experience budgeting, instruction, evaluation and other activities in which teachers, parents, and communities can be involved more fully;

4. the transfer of some central authority and responsibility:

   — down the system in order to encourage greater local control and autonomy and empower local communities and officials; and

   — out to other sectors, parents, community and professional associations, and NGOs;

5. the development of a new balance or 'hybrid' of powers among the various partners in education, with the centre assuming more the position of facilitator and enabler of participation of other levels and actors of the system, especially at the level of the school; and

6. the need to translate the rhetoric of participation into the practical reality of more participatory, collaborative approaches, both:

   — across all levels of the system (the community, local government, district offices, the central ministry, even donors, and

   — across the various types of personnel at each of these levels (i.e., including planners and technical officers).

To assist decision-makers, planners, and managers to promote such norms and encourage more participatory approaches to developing their education system requires several things:

— convincing them of the need for such approaches, while alerting them to their risks and to the difficulties in implementing them;

— getting them to assess the current nature, context, policies, and practice in regard to collaboration and participation in their systems;

— helping them to clarify the nation's goals in regard to such approaches;

— designing the mechanisms to encourage these approaches at all levels of the system;

— developing the strategies (policies, regulations, and guidelines) needed to implement such mechanisms; and

— training the persons concerned at various levels of the system in the knowledge, skills, and attitudes needed to put these strategies into place.

This chapter attempts to make a contribution in this regard by examining the nature of participatory approaches to development, their advantages and possible risks, the potential partners and the areas of possible collaboration in education, the conditions and factors conducive to such collaboration, and the ways in which such conditions can be encouraged in ministries of education.

Specifically, the mechanisms, the implementation strategies, and the training programmes needed to put such approaches into place. This includes first the development of teacher, parent, and community organizations as partners in educational development. Such organizations - teacher clubs, parent associations, PTAs, village education committees - are the basic building blocks of stronger school and community collaboration. Following the establishment of such organizations comes the facilitation of greater teacher, parent, and community involvement in specific areas of education. These areas include:

— the assessment of educational conditions, needs, priorities, and resources;

— policy-making and governance (the setting of goals, planning of programmes, and managing of budgets); and

— the instructional process.

The issues associated with participatory approaches to development are not neutral and 'value-free'. Rather, they are based on a number of assumptions which need to be taken into account while reading this chapter; namely that:

1. Participation is a 'good' in itself. The process of making decisions about one's own life and then acting on those decisions - of having some influence on the forces and pressures surrounding one's environment -brings benefits to individuals, communities, and society at large.

2. Participation has become a necessary, if not sufficient, aspect of development. Projects and programmes of development are likely to be more relevant, more supported, more successful, and more sustainable to the extent that they involve their 'targets' in their planning, implementation, and evaluation.

3. Participation and collaboration are not panaceas for educational underdevelopment. They cannot solve all problems, and they should not be used as a substitute for serious, systematic public attempts to plan, manage, and finance basic education more efficiently and with greater imagination. Above all, they should not be used as a excuse by government to get out of the 'business' of basic education.

4. Participatory and collaborative approaches are dependent on, and affected by, social, cultural, and political contexts. What works in one country may not work in another. These approaches therefore cannot be treated as recipes able to be implemented in the same way in all regions of the world. Rather, they should be seen as items on a menu of mechanisms, procedures, and administrative actions which can lead to a higher degree of participation in education, at both local and national levels. The choice of the items on the menu will vary by context and may very well change (perhaps even evolve towards the more participatory end of the range) over time. The specific nature of the items on the menu and of the suggested steps in their implementation will need to be adapted to the particular political, economic, educational and cultural context of each country. This chapter is therefore not meant to propose universal, standardized methods to promote collaboration and strengthen partnerships. Rather, it will suggest steps that need to be taken by central government officials in order to facilitate the implementation of such approaches both at their own level and at the local level.

5. Such approaches have disadvantages as well as benefits, costs as well as savings. They are often difficult to implement, can be risky as well as beneficial, and are not 'free'.

6. Based on considerable evidence of case studies and project reviews, under the right conditions, and given the right precautions, the greater participation of more actors can help improve the quality of, and the demand for, basic education.

As a final caution to planners and managers of development, including the author and readers of this chapter, this introduction ends with following quotes:

> "In the varied topography of professional practice, there is a high, hard ground overlooking a swamp. On the high ground, manageable problems lend themselves to solution through the application of research-based theory and technique. In the swampy lowland, messy, confusing problems defy technical solution. The irony of this situation is that the problems of the high ground tend to be relatively unimportant to individuals or to society at large, however great their technical interest may be, while in the swamp lie the problems of greatest human concern. The practitioner must choose. Shall he remain on the high ground where he can solve relatively unimportant problems according to prevailing standards of rigor, or shall he descend to the swamp of important problems and non-rigorous inquiry?" [Schon, Educating the reflective practitioner 1987, Bass].... More than most others, and more often - indeed daily - [the development profession] must deal with what Schon calls the "indeterminate zones of practice - uncertainty, uniqueness, and value conflict things which escape the canons of technical rationality".

> "It is perhaps because of our unconscious attachment to the norms of technical rationality, and our resistance to the messiness of the swamp, that it is difficult to cross over to quality in practice. We see that, in practice, popular participation is a messy business. So we spend much time breaking it down into its elements, and looking for mechanisms that will help in its promotion. Then, in frustration... we ask for 'how tos' If we were to break out of confines of technical rationality, in which we quite naturally take refuge, we might be freer to deal with the artistry that is needed in the swamp. In those 'indeterminate zones of practice', 'how tos', at least gene-ralizable ones, are by definition, not really possible to derive. We are talking about the art of development rather than the science of it".

Participatory Development

Popular participation consists of restoring the power of local people to take the initiative and the decision of formulating and implementing activities and programmes concerning their own future. It consists of recognizing that the people are creators and full-fledged partners in development. Promoting popular participation therefore means instituting a partnership, a contractual relationship among the various agents of development, in particular between the people concerned and those intervening from the outside. Whether the programmes are initiated from outside or in support of previously existing local initiatives, those intervening from outside should start off where the needs and aspirations of the people begin and accept to negotiate on that basis. If, as in many cases, such a partnership is initially held back by such factors as poor organization and improper formulation of requests for assistance, the conditions for the partnerships must be created.

A more participatory approach to development begins with the assumption that "sustainable development ultimately depends on enhancing people's capacities as individuals and groups to improve their own lives and to take greater control over their own destinies". This assumption may seem self-evident, but, in fact, it is really quite radical in implication. A participatory approach to development represents a considerable change in the process of governance, in social and political relationships, and in who participates in, controls, and is empowered by the development process.

The definitions given to terms associated with 'participation' have often remained vague, confusing, even contradictory. The distinction between 'participation' and 'involvement' is a case in point. One author in the field "argues for the primacy of participation ahead of involvement because "community participation means that the community has a right to be part of the action;...community involvement implies that the community is drawn into the action" ".

The World Health Organization, on the other hand, has said that "the term 'community involvement' has been given preference over 'community participation' because it is not sufficient merely to participate, which may be simply a passive response; there should be mechanisms and processes to enable people to become actively involved and to take responsibility for some decisions and activities jointly with health professionals".

Only recently has there been greater success in clarifying the definitions and essential characteristics of participatory development. An extensive discussion in development literature concerning participation of whom, in what, for what purpose, and to what degree - has helped greatly in this regard. As a result, several different degrees or definitions of participation in development can be described. One description, based on an early work by Arnstein, posits a 'ladder of participation', from non-participatory activities (manipulation, decoration, tokenism), to increasingly participatory activities where participants are 'assigned but informed', then consulted and informed, then share decision making in activities initiated by others, and then decide on and direct activities initiated by themselves.

A useful modification of this 'ladder' would describe degrees of participation as follows:

1. the mere use of a service (such as a primary health care facility);
2. involvement through the contribution (or extraction) of resources, materials, and labour;
3. involvement through 'attendance' and the receipt of information (e.g., at parents' meetings at school), implying passive acceptance of decisions made by others;
4. involvement through consultation (or feedback) on a particular issue;
5. participation in the delivery of a service, often as a partner with other actors;
6. participation as implementors of delegated powers; and
7. most completely, participation "in real decision-making at every stage identification of problems, the study of feasibility, planning, implementation, and evaluation". This implies the authority to initiate

action, a capacity for 'proactivity', and the confidence to get going on one's own.

The first four rungs of this ladder use the word involvement and, in agreement with Beare quote above, connote largely passive collaboration in development. In many societies, movement up these rungs - to the third or fourth rung (passive involvement in decision-making and in consultation and feedback) - would already represent considerable progress. Beyond such involvement, the last three items use instead the word participation, implying a much more active role, a role established by right. It is the last definition which is generally considered now as being that which underlies genuinely participatory development. Thus, people participate to the extent that they:

> "choose, cognitively, affectively, and physically, to engage in establishing, implementing, and evaluating both the overall direction of a programme and its operational details. Choice, in this context, implies not merely an agreement to follow but an active decision to assume responsibility in considering the rationale, implications and potential outcomes of the programme".

Such a definition requires people to have extensive influence on development decisions and therefore to have more than mere involvement in the implementation or benefits of development. It implies participation in the various stages of development activities:

— diagnosing and defining problems;

— collecting and analysing information;

— articulating priorities and setting goals;

— assessing available resources;

— deciding on and planning programmes;

— designing implementation strategies and apportioning responsibilities among participants;

— managing programmes;

— monitoring progress;

— evaluating results and impact; and

— redefining problems generated for further action.

Two important issues must be noted here.

— This definition represents a very ambitious goal - an ideal - likely unreachable (at least in the short-term) by many, if not most, societies of the world. The degree of participation able to be achieved in any given society, in other words, will need to be assessed realistically based on its level of development and its political, social, cultural, and economic context.

— Achieving greater participation in a society is an evolutionary process; it is "a long-term learning process and not a management tool".

A government bureaucracy, a community cooperative, a parent-teacher association do not suddenly, by fiat, become more participatory in nature, leaping from the first degree of participation to the last - or even to the middle. Rather, their willingness and ability to participate - and the feasibility of their doing so - evolve over time, faster or slower (perhaps with some backward steps), depending on a number of complex factors and conditions.

Having said this, however, it must be made clear that underlying all of the more participatory approaches to development are several important implications and issues that planners and managers as well as the political leadership of a government must understand. These all relate to the general process of the 'restructuring' of educational systems. This process represents a "significant change in the pattern of school governance, where governance refers to the norms and practices of decision-making regarding three critical areas of school life:

(1) instructional methodology and curriculum;

(2) administrative management and organization; and

(3) the generation, allocation, and use of resources".

Such restructuring generally includes issues related to decentralisation, accountability, autonomy, and empowerment.

Decentralization

The first relates to decentralization, a process often particularly crucial in any attempt to facilitate the participation of a broader range of actors in development. Decentralization is another concept, however, fraught with multiple and often contradictory variations. These include:

> Deconcentration, sometimes called administrative decentralization, involves handing over more routine authority and decision-making powers from a higher level of the central government to lower levels (regional, district, cluster), still accountable to, and staffed by, the central ministry.

Delegation transfers (or lends) certain specific management responsibilities for some activities to other units, governmental or non-governmental, implying somewhat stronger (but easily cancel-lable) local autonomy. Neither deconcentration nor delegation necessarily lead to more participatory approaches to development.

Privatisation is the divesting of functions to the private sector, to either voluntary or for-profit organizations. Devolution (sometimes called political decentralization) strengthens sub-national units of government and actually transfers considerable decision-making powers to local political bodies relatively independent of the central government. It is in the actual devolution of power to local lower-level bodies of government that the greatest scope for participatory development can be found. This strategy is meant to achieve various results:

1. to generate more resources and assure their more equitable allocation and effective use within the decentralized administrative units;
2. to improve the quality of decision-making and planning by making these processes more responsive to indigenous cultures and to local conditions, needs, and practices;
3. to speed up the decision-making process and free the centre to focus on its legitimate strategic concerns;
4. to encourage initiative, innovation, and participation;
5. to increase local responsibility and accountability over issues more readily understood by local management; and
6. to stimulate communication down and up the system of control.

But there are also problems with decentralization. It can lead to too much variety within a system and greater inequity across the system. The diversity and complexity of the services and policies which often result from decentralization make necessary more systematic and sophisticated monitoring and training of people working in such a system. And given the newly defined functions of powers of different levels of the system, decentralisation might require both careful planning and extensive training and more staff, resources, and equipment, rather than less. Thus, decentralization will not prove a cheaper form of management; its justification must be that it is better.

It has been argued that decentralization is often more rhetorical than real; that, as compensatory legitimation, it is designed to manage and diffuse conflict and fragment reform movements rather than bring about real change; and that if it involves only administrative aspects of a system, it can result in more rather than less central control as the administrative function becomes more efficient at the local level. Thus, decentralization of government in itself does not necessarily involve a devolution of power. Far from it, the extension of the state outwards and downwards can just as well serve the objective of consolidating the power of the central state as it can serve the objective of devolving power away from the centre.

Accountability

The second issue arising from more participatory development is accountability - another word that "continues to span a very wide variety of concepts and policies, making it an elusive concept to grasp".

Accountability relates to who is required to whom about - and therefore can ultimately be held responsible for the determination and implementation of policies and procedures, the achievement of goals, the performance of institutions, and compliance with standards and regulations.

At the most general and ideal level, this relates to the accountability of the "State and its agencies, institutions, and structures...to Civil Society". More specifically and realistically, in regard to participation and decentralization, it relates to the extent to which various levels of the administrative hierarchy are responsible to other levels both above and below it and to other 'partners'. In systems both decentralized and participatory, higher levels of the bureaucracy are to some extent accountable to lower levels (rather than only the other way around), and local government agents (e.g. the school and its staff) are to some extent accountable to their 'clients' (e.g. children, parents, the community) as well as to the local government office and the bureaucratic levels above. The question, answered differently according to the context, is how such accountability is put in place.

Autonomy

Societies where multidirectional accountability occurs guarantee some degree of autonomy or 'self-government' to lower levels of the system. This includes both autonomy for organizations to make and implement decisions regarding their own operations, and for individuals, to make decisions regarding matters pertaining to their own concerns. Such autonomy, within a context of accountability to other actors above and to clients below, can help to encourage better management, higher professional competence, and more effective services. One important premise of such a process of providing greater autonomy is that the various actors in the autonomous institutions (e.g. a school) are "professionals and able to make informed decision and conscious of self-responsibility for consequences arising from the decisions" —a premise which may need to be realized by better training of these actors.

Empowerment

One important outcome of more participatory processes will be empowerment. Greater participation in a decentralized system, with multiple and more democratic processes of accountability of more autonomous institutions, implies that people:

> gain knowledge and awareness of their own social, economic, and political conditions take action - to make and act on choices and to construct "their own futures through a process of analysis and action"; and, above all, gain control over the goals and processes of development, and over regulatory institutions. "If it is accepted that participation should start at the stage of conception and still be in evidence at the stage of supervision, then it is necessary to agree to share certain elements of power".

The concept of empowerment has become especially important in attempts to move the concept of participatory development from rhetoric to concrete practice. This concept is perhaps best defined as "a group process where people who lack an equal share of valued resources gain greater access to, and control over, those resources". As a result, "poor communities come more explicitly to assert rights and responsibilities in determining the direction of their own development".

This power must be real, formal, and legitimate, including both the ability to make use of formal structures and regulations and control over decision-making processes, knowledge, and techniques. People who are empowered "have the power to find direct solutions to their problems they propose solutions, they do not beg for them. What greater participation can achieve The interest in greater participation in development derives from the belief that such participation can achieve several goals, These include:

1. *ideological goals:* to empower people in order to ensure their greater control over development and their greater influence over decisions that affect them;
2. *economic goals:* both to seek more resources from a wider range of actors and to share the price of development by transferring some Costs from the 'suppliers' to the 'consumers';
3. *political goals:* from the government's side, to strengthen the legitimacy of the current government and make people co-responsible for social problems; from the 'popular' side, to gain greater share of power in policy-making and budget allocations;
4. *programmatic:* to increase programme or project demand, coverage, relevance, effectiveness, efficiency, success, and sustainability; and
5. *capacity-building:* to develop new knowledge, skills, and attitudes and provide beneficiaries a useful share in management tasks, monitoring, etc.

In general terms, a great part of the impact of participation and empowerment is said to lie at the level of the individual, in the process of "hum an resource development" . Some of this impact is cognitive. Through greater involvement in a variety of development activities, people can gain more knowledge, learn better practice, and end with a greater awareness of the development problems that exist, the causes behind these problems, and, in some cases, their possible solutions.

Some of the impact is also psychological; people feel greater self-confidence and self-reliance, less dependence on external inputs and 'wisdom', greater pride in the significance and validity of local knowledge and experience, a greater sense of accountability and responsibility for their own cations, less of a feeling of marginalisation and powerlessness. The combination of such impacts can lead to greater demand on the political and social system: people gain a better idea of the kind of life they want to lead, a greater understanding of what prevents them from achieving such a life, and a greater willingness to make their needs known and, when necessary, to play a larger role in fulfilling these needs themselves.

Much of the same kind of impact occurs at the community level as well. Communities can become less marginal and powerless, more self- reliant and independent, more accountable and responsible. Such communities can:

1. gain greater control over information and local technologies;
2. form alliances and networks within their own area or across to others;
3. work toward the more efficient and effective management of local resources and, in the longer term, greater ecological sustainability; and

4. develop skills, organisations, and a "corporate identity" which can serve them well, both in community development and as the basis for negotiating, from greater strength, with outside institutions and bureaucracies.

The result can be greater community cohesion; a more integrated process of "community learning" across formal, non-formal, and informal learning activities; greater economic development and cultural unity; and the assurance that local services - such as education - meet the needs, reflect the traditions and share the goals of the community.

In the best of circumstances, such achievements at the community level also benefit the society at large. Greater participation within a society can lower development costs, make development programmes more cost-effective, and ensure greater equity of the benefits of development within and across communities. It can also increase the impact and sustainability of development programmes by encouraging more of a "hand-crafted approach to development". With such an approach, utilisation rates, continuity, and maintenance of development programmes can be improved. Without such participation, the opposite may occur; thus, for example, "if the educational planners fail to consult the teachers before introducing reforms, they cannot but expect half-hearted support on the part of those concerned with their implementation".

Why it is difficult to 'do' participation

"For some participants the benefit of the participatory process is suspect; the participation involves people who have less skills or knowledge than those responsible for making decisions, are less accountable for whatever the outcome might be, or have a more self-interested level of involvement or concern than perhaps might be expected of the ultimate decision- makers. In these situations and for these people, participation is burdensome, an unwarranted cost, and does little to improve the quality of the eventual decision".

It is important to make clear that participation - and any accompanying devolution of authority and "empowerment of the masses" - should not be seen as a new panacea for underdevelopment. It is a difficult, frustrating process, sometimes risky and often unsustainable; both sceptics and advocates of participatory development recognize that it is a process fraught with disappointments, dangers, and unkept promises.

The difficulties of participation

Encouraging participatory approaches to development is difficult to do for several reasons.

— Many communities—perhaps especially those most disadvantaged—are not at all homogeneous in nature. Social stratification, divisions along caste, religious, and ethnic lines, personal rivalries and social factionalism, and the incompatibility of interests are all factors which make it difficult to talk of 'community' mobilisation through participation. A community seen as 'natural' in some ways (such as a caste) may not necessarily be the community most appropriate to mobilize towards a particular outcome (such as better sanitation), and a community defined by geography, perhaps most appropriate for improving a particular social service (such as sanitation), may be too riven with social discord to permit mobilisation. In such a context, participation may bring unresolved and unresolvable conflicts out into the open, exacerbating rivalries of class, caste, and ethnicity by making potential differences in goals and tactics explicit, rather than keeping them constrained and hidden through the operation of traditional roles and responsibilities.

— Even where community members may want to work together, a major obstacle may be the sheer lack of experience and skill in participatory and collaborative activities. Participation by the community in development and the collaboration of the community with other partners imply certain knowledge and skills: setting goals and priorities, running meetings, planning budgets, accounting for resources.

— Potential participants, especially those economically and socially weakest, may lack a sense of self-confidence and political efficacy -the feeling that "individual political action does have, and can have, an impact upon the policy process". They may also feel, or may have been encouraged to feel, that, given the overriding authority of the government, they have little political power, few obligations beyond receiving government services, and little ability to affect government policy.

— Marginal communities (and many governments) cannot bear the added expense of participatory processes - especially in terms of financial resources and of the time and energy required of participating community organisations, government agencies, and individuals. Overworked village leaders and community members struggling for survival, particularly if affected by the inherent passivity and illiteracy of many communities, do not find it easy to participate in labour-intensive, collaborative activities, and participation in the management of meagre resources is often seen as not worth the effort. And because sometimes "there are so many development agencies each dealing with problems in each sector, people can get only more and more confused because they do not have the training necessary to understand how all those activities which are being proposed willy-nilly to them tie into one another. The tendency is to set up village groups, associations, and committees each time a new operation commences. This has the double inconvenience of multiplying, at times needlessly, people's organizations and [of] marginalizing existing forms of organization with the result, in [some] cases, of creating social tension".

— Participatory processes do not just happen by themselves or by fiat, but rather require new and complex managerial and supervisory skills, attitudes, and behaviours. Principals able to share authority within and across schools, teachers (especially those from another region, ethnic group, or language group) able to carry out surveys of community needs, district officers able to work with programme staff of non-government organisations, central planners willing to issue the regulations mandating community involvement in curriculum development - all of these are not easy to develop in traditional bureaucracies and, once developed, to sustain. Sixth, participation is often in conflict with a political culture where initiatives toward reform may require clear sanction from above and where, for example, both parental participation in designing (let alone questioning) school policies and flexible, non-standardized responses to a variety of development contexts are difficult to imagine.

— Many institutions and individuals have a pro -found inability or resistance to change. The inertia of inflexible systems, bureaucratic delays, the lack of teamwork and co-ordinating mechanisms, the absence of clear rules as to who should do what and when, poor technical support from those meant to provide it, and the fear of losing control to other agencies, to lower levels of the system, or to outsiders - all make it difficult, at least early in various reforms, to encourage new initiatives. Thus, for example, reforms involving the participation of the community and of other sectors in education require flexible, multi-sectoral approaches and are often seen as interfering with the academic, examination-oriented aspects of the curriculum or as being intrusive, unprofessional, and working against the accepted wisdom that quality necessarily (and solely) depends on higher teacher salaries, better facilities, and the competence of a better teaching staff. Eighth, and finally, such problems are compounded by more concrete administrative obstacles. Logistical problems and staff turnover are notable in this regard; when staff trained in a more participatory approach and method are transferred or resign, much time and effort are wasted. Administrative procedures may also discourage collaboration. In some countries, for example, ministry regulations forbid parent associations from involvement in 'academic' matters, and in a number of countries more than one ministry may have responsibility for primary education. This can make any innovation, let alone that based on greater popular participation, difficult to implement.

The risks of participation

Participatory approaches to development can also carry risks. First, these approaches can raise expectations, and then frustrations, and lead to greater political and social instability. Participation can also threaten the political order of things. In simple terms, for example, "how many of the ruling elite would be comfortable with a critically conscious peasantry, and how many teachers with a body of [students] who are developing critical consciousness?". The result may be suspicion and fear among the elite and repression of the population. Such approaches can also mislead marginal populations, who have little margin for risk, into taking risks and then failing, with possible disastrous effects. And the lack of technical expertise, supervisory skills, and animaters and of a participatory grassroots tradition in many societies can lead to failed projects and a decline in the quality of services provided.

Second, the participatory process may place greater power in the hands of the 'wrong' people - factionalists, demagogues, racists, reactionaries. It can also be taken over by those parts of any community - i.e., often corrupt and inefficient local elites and party cadres - most able (financially and personally) to 'participate'. These groups may use their increased authority to manipulate the 'participants' and extract further resources from them. Attempt to encourage community involvement in development may therefore lead instead to the promotion of people who speak only for given segments of the population. It is they, rather than the "poorest of the poor", who benefit. The result may be an unequal distribution of participation itself and of its benefits either of the direct benefits meant to be derived from the new service or of the more generalized benefits of involvement in the development process.

Third, a further risk of participatory processes may be the domination, at the local level, of narrow community self-interest, which may be based on short-sighted perspectives and aim at short-term benefits. Such self-interest may ignore longer-term political or economic implications for the community or the larger society and contradict more general goals of national integration, the dissemination of scientific truth, and the modernisation of society. In education, for example, local communities participating in the support and governance of schools may believe that these schools belong to them and have little responsibility to deliver more nationally-oriented messages. This may lead to undue interference in school management or the demand for favours in return for donations and support (Commonwealth Secretariat 1992). Also, 'popular' traditions and customs in areas such as health, nutrition, productivity, or social justice may, in fact, represent "developmentally inadequate practices and behaviour" which should not be reinforced in development programmes or reflected in local social services.

Fourth, another problem lies in the risk of tokenism - only marginal change, wrapped in new packaging, leading not to an alternative model of development but rather to the reinforcement of central power and the reproduction of central values. Participation, in other words, may end up being 'system-maintaining', designed to "transform disadvantaged and disaffected groups into 'responsive citizens' implementing policies outlined by some higher authority", rather than 'system-transforming', designed to "effectively transfer political and economic power to hitherto disadvantaged groups and thus to introduce more radical social change". Attention paid and energy spent by the general population on such token achievements are then lost to attempts to change more fundamentally the basic political and administrative patterns of a society . The process of change therefore becomes de politicized.

Likewise, the very public efforts to wrap the new package in an attractive cover of 'participation' can lead to a fifth risk - the opting out of government from its responsibilities for delivering basic social services and for the better management, or more equitable allocation, of resources. In some countries, rather than maintaining their monopoly on the education system as omnipotent planner and funder, governments are moving in the opposite direction - surrendering their (expensive) responsibility for basic education to the family and the community. This may end up with the government co-opting NGOs and other community-based associations into State mechanisms and bureaucratic processes. Governments may even be able to blame poor results and poor quality on the other 'partners'; the more actors involved, in other words, the more blame can be distributed and the less the government itself can be held accountable.

The uncertainties of participation

In addition to the difficulties and risks of more participatory processes in development, there are also considerable uncertainties about it. First is the sheer inability to know, and to show to others, when a participatory process has succeeded. Participation is a process and, as described above, its products are often psychological, procedural, or organisational in nature rather than concrete in terms of money saved or services delivered. "As a process, participation evolves at its proper pace and rhythm, adapted to the people involved rather than to bureaucratically or politically defined projects or goals. It may go in unforeseen directions and may not in the short term have an immediately quantifiable or measurable impact". The lack of process indicators and measures means that success is easy to claim but difficult to substantiate.

A second problem relates to the inability to standardize or generalize the implementation of participatory development due to the different configurations of participation in various regions of the world and even in different parts of a country. To the extent that participation is not an 'intervention' per se, that culture, history, and government policy affect its success, and that it is a dynamic process which requires flexibility, it is very much situation-specific. In other words, there cannot be a standard recipe for achieving participatory development; what makes it 'work' varies tremendously across different economic, political, and cultural contexts.

There are many reasons for such variety: different histories of development, different social relationships and cultural traditions related to participation, and different political constraints or freedoms. Thus, schools and communities may respond in quite different ways to regulations concerning collaboration, and the nature of such collaboration and the kinds of structures which might encourage it differ across urban, suburban, and rural contexts. Attempts to develop manuals, guidelines, and training materials related to participatory approaches must therefore be tempered by their extensive adaptation to local conditions.

Despite these problems, however, participatory approaches to development have proven instrumental, in particular contexts and under particular conditions, in expanding the supply and increasing the relevance of basic social services and in enhancing people's capacities as individuals and as groups to improve their own lives and to take greater control over their own development. This occurs most readily, of course, under two conditions:

(1) that the users of this approach recognize, and move to control, the possible negative aspects of participation described above, and

(2) that the dominant actor in development - the government—is committed, at all levels, to working more collaboratively with, and encouraging the greater participation of, other partners in development.

Participatory approaches in education

Development of participatory approaches in education includes the broader and active partnerships both inside the system at the central level and in the school and the greater collaboration of educational personnel and the external community in planning, managing, and implementing educational programmes. The potential partners are many: teachers, headteachers, and local educational officials; parents and members and leaders of the local community; community associations and non-government organizations (NGOs); private enterprises and universities. Before discussing where and how greater collaboration among such partners can more readily occur, it is necessary to understand clearly the characteristics of these major actors.

Although bureaucracies - in education ministries as well as in other sectors - may be effective managers of top-down development projects and programmes and may have a range of human and material resources, an extensive infrastructure, and administrators and experts who bring to their work considerable knowledge, skills, and experience, they also may possess several characteristics which work against more participatory approaches to development. Limited knowledge of, or sensitivity to, community conditions and local experience. Older educational administrators often may have started their careers as teachers but then worked many years in various parts and at various levels of the ministry structure, far from the everyday reality of schools and communities. While some younger ones may have teaching experience, many may have moved directly into ministry positions following university or college training. Their experience has largely been gained, therefore, in academic or office settings rather than in the field. The experience of both kinds of administrators, only reinforced by their position within the central bureaucracy, may produce a particular view of development. In reference to another sector, but relevant as well to education, one observer describes a common perception among government managers that "all knowledge, the necessary clinical skills and insights, the right strategies, the right perceptions of the health problems at the local area, all supposedly reside at the centre of the centralized system". One effect of this perception can be a particular set of attitudes toward the 'periphery'. This includes:

— the retaining of firm control over the development process by the centre with full confidence that the periphery will implement the centres decisions as required;

— the assumption that lower levels of the bureaucracy are capable merely of implementing policies and decisions made at the top;

— little appreciation of (or even scorn for) local or indigenous knowledge or creative potential of what are seen as largely passive 'beneficiaries', especially in comparison with the supposed expertise of professionals in the centre;

— little recognition of the potential or achievements of local institutions; and

— a kind of 'cultural arrogance' that none of these institutions could be more or less equal in collaboration for development.

One author describes these 'centre' attitudes in very clear terms:

> "One often hears the city people talk in contempt about the village people. They call the masses lazy, ignorant, conservative, fatalistic, even stupid....They have no respect for the wisdom of the masses, for the wealth of their experience. They do not realise that the masses have managed to survive and keep the economics of [their] countries going not because of the help of the city people, but in spite of their exploitation by the moneyed and landed urban and rural elites".

A top-down mentality "based on transmitting instructions from above, giving orders to people below them, strictly obeying instructions received (or making a show of it) and making the boss happy". Vertical communication, when it exists, flows down such a structure, from the top to the bottom, with few opportunities for the reverse. This can lead to:

— the discouragement and even the fear of diversity and local initiative;

— the avoidance of open consultation and interaction, except with other professionals speaking the same language;

— the desire to control information, events, and people;

— a resistance to change in structures or procedures; and, ultimately,

— the principle motivation of the public servant and the expert being the maintenance and control of the status quo.

Centralized, standardized, and routinized governmental structures and procedures, based on departmental, sectoral, and/or disciplinary lines which make difficult any attempts to respond flexibly to particular local conditions and needs and to integrate development efforts. Thus, although, "the geographical dispersion of schools and the organisational tradition of teacher independence in the classroom give education all of the characteristics of a decentralized enterprise, [yet] in most developing countries the education system is hierarchically structured, with most of the important decisions made by central government ministries".

The result is often an attempt "to enclose people in standardized rules, regulations, and official institutions, thereby discouraging voluntary initiatives and promoting apathy, withdrawal and often passive resistance". Limited financial and human resources necessary to penetrate regularly and systematically, even through what is often an extensive network of local offices, to all of a country's villages and settlements, let alone to those most isolated and marginal. With such a limited reach, governments may be hard-pressed to implement the standardized policies they often seek to promote, let alone react flexibly to the particular needs of diverse communities. These limitations may be particularly acute in increasingly expensive and complex educational systems where central governments attempt with great difficulty to control the daily life of literally thousands of schools. Inflexible procedures of planning, decision-making, implementation, evaluation, accountability, etc. These can lead to the design of quick solutions to complex problems, the rapid assessment of quantifiable output, and the desire for immediate success. In such a system, there may be little exploration of alternative approaches and little advantage seen in attempts to encourage messier, more complex, and potentially less immediately and less visibly successful activities. This generally rigid approach is often reinforced by the importance given to national goals of unity and integration and by the necessity imposed by both internal auditors and external funders for detailed planning and budget cycles, work schedules, and target dates.

Such pressures can make it difficult to adapt to local circumstance and therefore tempt a ministry to finish a given project, declare it a success, and move to yet another rather than reinforcing the operations, maintenance, and sustainability of the first. This approach has been called the 'blueprint approach', reflecting "the textbook version of how development programming is supposed to work...with...clear-cut orders, allocation of funds for precisely-stated outcomes, reliance on 'hard' data and expert judgement, and the clearly-stated implementation schedules which make project justification easy in budget presentations".

In such a system, evaluation of staff performance may be based on the number of development projects completed or the amount of budget spent rather than the extent of local capacity developed, and personnel end up being accountable solely to superiors within the bureaucracy and not to the so-called beneficiaries. And as long as members of the bureaucracy "remain unconvinced that they need the willing co-operation of local-level people to improve their performance in ways significant to their careers, they are unlikely to facilitate 'animation techniques' and they may well sabotage them".

The particular weakness of the intermediate (regional, district, sub-district) level of government. This level is necessarily a crucial actor in any kind of educational change, especially given the variety of important roles it can play. These include:

— providing professional assistance and technical support to schools and their personnel,

— promoting the exchange of information across schools,

— mediating and channelling communication between the top and the bottom and passing information both up and down the system,

— participating in the selection, placement, and promotion of teachers and principals, and given its links to a community beyond that of a particular school (e.g., intermediate-level offices of other development sectors such as health and agriculture), connecting the school to this wider range of potential partners and resources.

But such levels of the system - even more than central levels - tend to be inadequately staffed, poorly financed, and limited (often willingly) in their authority to act.

"The typical district office operates...solely as a 'mailbox', transmitting guidelines, decisions, and rules from the central offices down to the lower layers of the administrative machinery.... There are no incentives to encourage the intermediate levels to mismanagement, violation of rules, or, on the other hand, the good performance of institutions, requiring rewards or encouragement. Nor are there incentives for the intermediate levels to promote, at the lower levels of the system, initiatives, innovative attitudes, or educational experiments with a risk element".

The school: heads and teachers

The school, as the major actor in educational development, is composed of both teachers and managers. Both are included in this heading, though their roles in various contexts are often quite different. In some systems, head teachers are seen as the lowest end of the government bureaucracy, trusted to carry out its administrative tasks and deliver its educational instructions to teachers; they therefore tend to share many of the characteristics of the government administrators described above. In other contexts, however, headteachers are seen more as senior teachers—above all responsible for pedagogical issues, with administrative tasks added on, but generally treated in the same way as teachers by the bureaucracy.

Though there is, of course, a huge variety of conditions in schools within and across countries of the developing world, there are certain common characteristics of schools of poorer countries and for marginal and disadvantaged populations. A quote from a study of rural Chilean schools portrays such conditions:

> "The poverty of the schools in the sample is striking. In addition to being located in poor neighbourhoods, in the case of the urban schools, and in isolated rural areas, the school buildings are visibly deteriorated. Peeling walls, flimsy construction material and unfinished classrooms, permeated by the smell of bathrooms without running water. Playgrounds are generally dirt-covered, treeless, and two narrow to run or play freely in. In southern Chile, some of the playgrounds have roofs to protect the children in winter, which makes them dark and enclosed..." "In the classrooms, there are rows of broken and worn-out desks, the wrong size for different ages, some collapsed and useless, piled in a corner; windows are often patched with paper for want of glass, the floor cracked or simply dirt-covered. Most classrooms are cold, dark, small and barely isolated from outside noise. Blackboards are not always painted black or dark green for better visibility and are often worn out, grey or pale green smudged with poor quality chalkdust. Few of the schools visited have a room where children can consult books outside class hours or when they need information for an assignment. In some schools, the principals had students leafing through dictionaries in their offices.

Teachers' rooms also lack conditions for rest periods or team work. They are small and frequently lack enough seats, coa-tracks or hangers, or shelf space for books and materials. Teachers go in and out between classes, but it is clearly not easy to teach and learn in these conditions. Some children erase the first pages in their notebooks in order to write on them again. Some children go around the class trying urgently to borrow a pencil to do an assignment. The teachers seem tired, even at the beginning of the school day. Many of them come from other schools where they work in the morning. They are modestly dressed and often look as poor as their pupils. The men teachers, only one or two in the lowest grades, wear shabby suits or well-worn sports clothes. Some of the women teachers wear smocks over their clothes, but, like the children lining up before class, their clothes reveal them as impoverished professionals, disciplined in the rituals of the school and the recent history of silence and authoritarianism that is only just beginning to change". In this and many other settings typical problems include the following:

> Shortages of books and materials and inadequate or deteriorating facilities. Many schools in many countries of the world suffer from the lack or complete absence of even the minimum facilities and materials for eduction. Underpaid, overworked, and demotivated teachers. Many teachers must work with insufficient and irregularly paid salaries, poor promotion opportunities and living conditions, the burden of excess subject content, reduced prestige, and either low enrolment and often absent pupils or overcrowded classrooms.

"Nearly everywhere [teachers] suffer from a sense of grievance. One reason for this is that their rates of pay are usually not so favourable as those of many others who have received the same amount of education. Another reason in many countries is that their prestige, which once was high in rural areas when they were the only educated person, has inevitably slumped with the spread of education".

The result can be heavy teacher absenteeism, an erosion of self-confidence (and of community confidence in teachers), a feeling of non-accountability to parents and the community, and a general decline in respect. This can all lead to a lack of teacher involvement as 'interior' actors in the school. Lack of competence, experience, and authority of headteachers and other supervisors. Heads of schools, as well as supervisors and inspectors, are often chosen more for seniority of tenure (and nearness to retirement) than for expertise and thus may have neither the knowledge nor the status to assist their colleagues professionally. Mechanisms of teacher support, let alone of administrative or pedagogical consultation, are therefore often weak.

The ambiguous position of teachers and headteachers. Both teachers and head teachers are much like a kind of 'extension agent' of the Ministry, facing many of the particular dilemmas of such agents in other departments. Are they merely part of an 'extended elite', representing the top of the bureaucracy to the bottom? Are they go-betweens and mediators between top and bottom? Or are they champions of the communities and populations in which they work? In other words, do they consider themselves to be primarily accountable to the bureaucracy above them or to the community below? A lack of clear answers to these questions puts many teachers into difficult, ambiguous, even conflictual situations.

The isolation and indifference of teachers. One result of such ambiguity is that teachers often consider themselves masters or mistresses of their classrooms, fully trained and certified, and therefore feeling little responsibility for the failure of their pupils and little interested either in receiving advice from superiors or in sharing experience with peers. For a similar reason, they also often 'disqualify' the experience of parents, especially those from low-income, marginal, and minority ethnic groups, and reject or even fear their involvement in school, having the attitude that parents, generally 'unaware' of the benefits of education, should 'surrender' their children to the school from the age of six or seven and thereafter not get involved in its activities.

Some teachers have considerable knowledge of their pupils, of the local environment and of what is feasible and useful in the context of the local school. There are many so-called 'high involvement' teachers who "equate professionalism with the ability to maintain a dialogue between the in- and out-of-school lives of both their students and themselves". But many others are 'low-involvement' teachers for whom:

> "being a professional means separating and protecting their work with students from thoughts, experiences, and people beyond the classroom walls....Not only do low involvement teachers maintain themselves in a position that is distant and autonomous from parents, they also envision themselves in an authoritarian position in relation to the mothers. The low involvement teachers deal with parents hierarchically, as though the parents are not as smart, not as moral, or not as worthwhile. Furthermore, to the low involver, there is a superior status that rightfully belongs to teachers - a sense of entitlement that the low involvers convey when they talk about teaching: entitlement to respect, trust, and irreproachability".

Getting such teachers more actively involved in school, as interior participants in educational change, may be particularly difficult. The 'loosely coupled' nature of schools in relation to the larger education system. While schools are part of a network of central, regional, and local interests and are heavily dependent on complementary institutions and subsystems (training colleges, examination systems, curriculum development centres), they are often only weakly linked, at the end of a long chain of command, to this bureaucracy. This makes problematic both their constructive input to any reform process and the relevance and feasibility of any decision made by the top about the bottom - and thus imperils the success of any central and standardized reform at the school level.

The nature of the 'community' and of the conditions which determine its fate are perhaps even more varied than those of the 'school'. Communities can be defined by law and geography, culture and language, class and caste, 'interest' and 'attachment'. They can be heterogeneous or homogeneous, united or conflictive, poor or rich, sunk in fatalism or vibrant with optimism (and the last are not necessarily correlated with levels of prosperity). They can be governed and managed by leaders chosen democratically (informally or through formal channels) and acting relatively autonomously from other levels of government, or by leaders imposed from above and representing central authorities.

Such leaders may either serve as effective catalysts between development agencies and the local population, or be loathe to let loose their traditional and often monopolistic hold on local communities. Many communities, also, especially in disadvantaged areas, lack cohesive, homogeneous social units and even informal local organisations which might be mobilized for greater participation. Others may have quite active local associations (e.g., for women and youth, for cooperative economic and cultural activities, and for religious and political purposes). Each of these characteristics will influence the degree to which communities themselves, their leaders, and any existing community-based associations are involved - or are able and willing to be involved - in development and in education.

In general, especially in socially and economically marginal regions, communities are not deeply involved as external actors in formal education. Depending on the nature of the community, this may be also true for parents of children in school. There are several reasons for this:

1. a lack of the time, energy, and sense of 'efficacy' required for such involvement;
2. a lack of appreciation of the overall objectives of education and a mismatch between what parents expect of education and what the school is seen as providing;
3. the belief that education is essentially the task of the State;
4. the length of time required to realise the benefits of better schooling;
5. ignorance of the structure and functions of the school;
6. the school's disinterest or resistance to community or parental involvements in what are often seen as specialized and professional matters; and
7. an underestimation by parents of their own competence in educational issues and the fear of being blamed for their children's 'backwardness'.

The involvement of parents and the community in school is largely extractive in nature; that is, community participation is limited to the provision of resources - money, materials, labour. Other, more substantial involvement in terms of consultation or management or control -in the diagnosis of needs, the development and implementation of school policies, the design of educational content, or the delivery or evaluation of such content - is usually seriously constrained.

But communities often have strengths of their own-energy, resources, knowledge, and experiences - rarely used in centrally-and bureaucratically -determined development programmes. "That the rural poor continue to survive under the most extremely unfavourable circumstances is testimony to the fact that they possess a good deal of technical and social knowledge relevant to their condition - knowledge of which many a university trained technician may be unaware. The best solution to any given village level problem is likely to be one to which both the technician and the villager have contributed their respective knowledge".

More involvement in education might therefore permit families and communities to accept that: "their accountability in the education of children extends beyond the provision of material requirements for schooling; that it includes the main responsibility of assisting, guiding, and extending whatever help their children need to harness their potential; and that they equally share the burden of education children with the teachers"

Non-Government Organisations (NGOs)

NGOs see development "not merely as an activity geared towards producing a certain output but as a process of developing community motivation and awareness, of promoting peoples abilities so that they can help themselves and, in turn, create a self-reliant community and nation". Governments often see NGOs as "being unprofessional, dogging, poorly organized, non-comprehending gaggles of usually undisciplined, if well-meaning, civilians".

In 1987 $2.2 billion (or 5 per cent) of the world's official development assistance was provided by donors to non-government organisations; another $3.3 billion was added to this total through NGO efforts. This considerable sum and percentage have no doubt increased over the last few years. As NGOs play an increasingly large role in the collection and distribution of development assistance, their involvement in the planning and delivery of development programmes also mounts. There is no universally accepted definition or classification of NGOs (or PVOs - private voluntary organisations - as they are often called). Some classifications include under one label organisations ranging from small village-level associations through national institutions operating in thousands of villages to international agencies with hundreds of staff and dozen of regional and national branches.

Others distinguish between grassroots organisations of the poor and 'popular' sectors (such as peasant movements, tribal associations, women's clubs, and labour unions) and more 'intermediate' agencies or non-government development organisations (NGDOs)—'nonprofit private organisations staffed by (semi)professionals who are engaged, full-time, in the design and implementation of grassroots development projects and programmes with and for the poor in the third world'. Yet other classifications include profit-making organisations, foundations, churches and missions, medical organisations and hospitals, unions and professional organisations, business and commercial enterprises, and co-operatives and cultural groups.

NGOs can also be classified as "sectoral, integrative, action-oriented, research-based, educational bodies, policy organizations, politically focused, or any combination of the above". Another typology distinguishes among conformist, reformist, and transformist or emancipatory organizations. Others would insist that NGOs be seen very much as public rather than private institutions - as "part of the public domain of governance by Civil Society".

Recent literature has developed more precise classifications of NGOs through an analysis of their evolution. In one kind of analysis, NGOs have developed from agencies primarily concerned with relief, welfare, and service delivery activities, to those encouraging small-scale, self-reliant local development projects and processes, to those more directly involved with community empowerment and social transformation.

Further evolution has led to two other categories. One is the type of large, umbrella, 'policy-advocacy' NGO, which forms networks or federations of advocacy organizations and develops distinct social, political, and economic functions and influence within the policy-making processes of a country. Another is the 'service provider' organisation which sees its role more in terms of supporting, protecting, linking, and developing the capacity of a myriad of action-oriented but often weak and relatively powerless grassroots NGOs - "more in the manner of a foundation, directing its attention to facilitating development by other organizations, both public and private, of the capacities, linkages, and commitments required to address designated needs on a sustained basis".

Such diversification of roles should not obscure a general commonality of characteristics and functions. In ideal terms, NGOs are most often described as people-centred, flexible and responsive, creative, democratic and non-hierarchical, cost-effective and pragmatic, with rather large margins for error, and often independent and nonaligned. They generally develop as the result of community support, are able to tap local knowledge and resources, and usually have a small core of paid staff and (often) many volunteers.

But NGOs may also have quite rigid and bureaucratic structures (perhaps the result of too much success) and be understaffed and poorly managed, with limited financial accountability, a lack of professional training, a concern for only short-term change and a narrowly-defined clientele, and an agenda closely tied to political ends and organizations. Whatever their characteristic, NGOs generally seek to carry out several functions:

> providing development services in those fields, activities, or regions either underserved by government or parallel to those provided by the government, often with greater effectiveness and equity. More and more frequently, they also work directly with governments (and sometimes with donors) in the provision of services, often as an intermediary between government agencies and the poorest levels of society; experimenting and testing new approaches to development and service delivery; increasingly, within individual countries and internationally through networks and federations, exploring new issues of social concern

> and serving as advocates and 'noise-makers' in regard to issues such as the environment and health, human rights, women's issues, and peace, and helping to build consensus and initiate policy change around such issues empowering the poor and the oppressed and building and strengthening people's organisations and community associations; and "strengthening civil Society in its relationships vis-a-vis the State and the ruling elites" by re-energising and rejuvenating social movements; promoting democratic practices and processes; and encouraging citizen engagement with public policy issues.

Given these functions and characteristics, there can easily be a clash of organisational norms and cultures between government and aid agency bureaucracies and non-governmental organisations - a clash which can often lead to a dversarial relationships and to government intimidation and regulation. One problem is the differing unit of activity the discrete, defined, elaborately planned and budgeted, and carefully timed 'project' of governments and aid agencies versus the more interactive, unbounded, often vaguely-defined and open-ended 'process' of NGOs.

Other problems include the sheer distance among the various actors -social, ethnic, political, cultural, even geographic; differences in perceptions, working styles, personalities, and approaches; hidden agendas and previous negative experiences; even a difference in salaries (donor, government, NGO) among those meant to be working as equals. And there is ingrained suspicion between the various ' sides' . Governments believe NGOs encourage division and sow discord between the people and government agencies, expose government shortcomings, and confuse people concerning government aims.

They fear that too much NGO criticism of the policies and programmes of the State might weaken it in relationships with foreign countries and donors. And they feel that NGO activities, by raising questions concerning economic distribution, social control, and the accountability of power -and even the very models and frameworks of development in use - are a challenge to State authority; this may particularly be the case in one-party states where the party itself is seen as the 'voice of the people' and therefore the channel through which all community-level work should flow.

NGOs, on the other hand, often believe that government officials and bureaucracies are inefficient, cautious, and slow, with a limited capacity for intellectual and technical inputs, more interested in personal gain than social welfare, dominated by corruption, biased toward support to the elites and other civil servants, and ignorant of the real problems of the people. The result of all of these factors can be jealousy, the inability or unwillingness to seek compromise or clarify respective responsibilities, and the taking of refuge in technical approaches by government and in ideological rhetoric by NGOs. NGOs also have fears concerning their links with governments:

— the fear that increased funding of NGOs may lead towards the privatisation of services to the poor and thus the withdrawal of the State from its social responsibilities;

— the risk that the increasing co-ordination of NGOs, either through government regulation or donor preference, might harm their principal focus on decentralized, community-based initiatives;

— the belief that more frequent legislation and regulation concerning NGOs in the developing world may cripple rather than support their activities; and

— the belief that as NGOs become subcontractors for development programmes designed and funded by others they will lose their role as creative, responsive actors in their own right.

This last is the fear of some NGOs of the possibility of dependency and co-optation—that too close an approach to government on the part of NGOs, and too great an acceptance of funding from national governments and international donors, will make them lose their identity and their (often) hard-won autonomy. But others fear that if NGOs are too small in scale, they become insignificant; if too independent, powerless; if too low-cost, of low quality; and if too innovative, temporary and unsustainable. NGOs therefore need to "learn to sup with a long spoon and to balance co-operation and confrontation in their dealings with officialdom".

Given the usual (and often limited) patterns of interaction among the various actors in education at the school and community level, the complexities and potential disadvantages of greater participation described above, and the quite profound differences between government agencies and non-government organisations, it should be clear why it can be difficult to develop and maintain collaboration and genuine partnerships in education. The technocratic, centralized, uniform, supposedly 'scientific' authority usually imposed by the State - with all of its related values, priorities, and approaches - is not easily wed to, or even tolerant of, the more culturally-based, decentralized, diverse, supposedly traditional authority derived from the 'people'.

Such differences are reflected in differing views of how schools can best be managed:

> "Those who champion democratic participation in education believe that communities will be served best when decision-making is decentralized and when people - teachers, parents, and students alike - are encourage d to participate directly in making the decisions that affect them....In contrast to this view, the notion of administrative leadership is one which implies hierarchical elevation of the...principal to an extraordinary level of power, centralising decision-making and control of resources in the hands of the few....It is assumed that strong leaders, with their expertise, technical know-how and experience, can solve administrative problems more efficiently than could cumbersome and wasteful community participation in decision-making".

The ideal compromise between such views would accept the need for some kind of central government authority and framework to:

1. establish common goals, general policies, and national planning processes;
2. determine basic curricular content and uniform achievement standards;
3. guarantee basic inputs;
4. collect basic system statistics and evaluate educational outcomes;
5. compensate for imbalances across schools and regions; in other words, "co-ordinate local action, reconcile divergent interests and project the weak, the losers, and, sometimes, minorities".
6. serve as the principal negotiator and communicator "in an educational landscape featuring many

decision-making centres both in and out of government"; and

7. plan for and explore the long-term future through enrolment and flow projections, the programming of public investment, the generation of scenarios to assess the consequences of policy changes, etc.

At the same time this hybrid would recognize the right of school personnel, local authorities, and the popular sectors to adapt and implement the national framework and fill it with local content. It would encourage a distribution of power in which each side has an equal opportunity to influence the other, and it would respect the traditional wisdom of local communities, the experience of teachers and principals, and the legitimacy of non-government organisations. It would also encourage the exchange of experiences, information, techniques, approaches, and resources among government offices, NGOs, and community groups.

Most importantly, perhaps, this ideal partnership would see the usual 'controllers' of development - governments and the donors which support them - rather as the 'enablers' of development. They would be charged with permitting other actors, from the bottom up, to assume both the rights and the risks of being partners in educational development and with "preserving, protecting, opening or creating necessary 'spaces' - political, legal, social, economic, and cultural - for participation to emerge and thrive".

An ideal partnership would also help facilitate participation by these actors (e.g., through parent training programmes), in order not only to share responsibility with them for the failure of projects and programmes, but also to build the capacity of otherwise marginal groups in assessing needs, designing and managing programmes, and making decisions. Finally, it would reduce the "constraints to local initiatives imposed by absolute and unresponsive administrative forms"; guarantee enough autonomy at the local level to encourage school and community partnerships in formulating, implementing, and evaluating school improvement programmes; and search for the optimal, if ever-changing, mix of centralized and decentralized structures and procedures. In more concrete terms, such a mix might see central governments retaining responsibility for establishing:

— a core curriculum;

— standards of financial accountability;

— minimum levels of teacher qualification and compensation;

— a minium number of schools days per year; and

— minimum levels of centrally-provided school financing.

Transferred further down or out of the system might then be such items as curricula design, the publishing and/or procurement of textbooks, and the production of locally-relevant teaching and learning materials; the collection and management of local resources; adjustments to the school calendar; inspection and supervision; and the hiring, training, and promoting of teachers. The case of the State of Victoria in Australia illustrates one such mix of powers. There are several important implications of such a 'centralized-decentralized' hybrid.

— The need to decentralize from a position of strength - in other words, from a relatively strong central system. "Central strength based on anemic [local] institutions is an illusion; and it is also unlikely that there can be effective [local] institutions in the absence of strong central support". This requires that the divisions of labour and responsibilities among various levels are clearly understood and the systems of communication and up and down the system, are clearly established; that local administrative units clearly have (or are provided) the management capacity to handle the functions transferred; and that the necessary resources (financial and otherwise) can be provided to these units to make them viable and productive.

— It is in this context that the role of the mediating institution often becomes important. If it is accepted that the "State represents macro, aggregated, cumulated formations and structures in a country [and] as a result, State policies, agencies, officials operate at a level far more macro than the level of the family", then the relations between the State and the family often need to be mediated, especially in more coercive or totalitarian contexts. In some cases very local organizations such as community or neighbourhood associations, churches, and voluntary organisations can play such a role; in others, stronger, more organized NGOs (local, national, international) may help to ensure such mediation and thus guarantee the balance of power between the family and the State.

— Such a mix or partnership in education implies the increased participation in school both of teachers and of parents and the community (directly or via community associations and NGOs). There will be a variety of patterns of such participation, depending on the context, with some partners having only input into some issues (e.g., curriculum, administrative decisions) and others having final authority over these issues. But no matter what the pattern, the important point is that a more collaborative partnership should be developed. Finally, this hybrid of responsibility requires a greater emphasis on school-based management, where individual schools have considerable autonomy in decision-making. In such management, "the school becomes the principal entity of any change in the educational system. It is the epicentre for the implementation of educational reforms". This, in turn, requires "the sharing of responsibilities among all those who participate in the life of the school".

CHAPTER 4

Diverse Learners in a Multicultural Society

With the rapidly changing population demographics of the United States and the significant growth of diverse multicultural groups, schools and professionals are being challenged as to how to provide the best comprehensive educational and support services to their increasingly diverse student population. The increasing diversity within the schools is also demonstrated by the higher visibility of other groups of diverse learners, including, but not limited to, children with disabilities, children and families identified with the deaf culture, and gay and lesbian youth.

The challenges in working with an ever growing pluralistic school population encompass many areas. The provision of relevant multicultural curriculums, the use of culturally sensitive assessment and intervention strategies, the training of school staff in the provision of these services, the recruitment and retention of multicultural and diverse professionals, and the integration of diverse communities and parents in an authentic and empowering manner are only a few of the critical issues facing those working with today's students.

Professionals are also challenged by the need to consider the impact of complex social/environmental problems, which in many contexts have negative consequences for children from various racial/ethnic and social class backgrounds. Only a few of these major issues will be highlighted.

Although there has clearly been a greater recognition of the need for training in multicultural competence across professions, many programs still conceptualize this training as more of an "add-on"; that is, programs require only one or two courses for their particular professional specialty. This is in contrast to a more comprehensive and integrated "paradigm shift" in the teaching of all helping professional courses.

The training of school staff and other related professionals can be conceptualized by using a model that emphasizes three major components: awareness, knowledge, and skills.

The awareness component involves professionals examining their own values, myths, stereotypes, and world view. Knowledge entails developing a non-stereotyping, flexible understanding of cultural, social, and family dynamics of diverse groups, along with a comprehension of the critical sociopolitical, historical, and economic contexts in which people from diverse multicultural groups are embedded.

Skills require the development of culturally sensitive, flexible, and empowering treatment and assessment strategies that are accompanied by communication skills, the integration of multicultural and diversity issues in various treatment modalities, multicultural consultation, and advocacy skills.

Depending on the school, staff, and community context, flexible training can take place on many levels, such as formal multicultural issues course work, in-service training, long-term consultation and analysis, multicultural program development, and reciprocal relationships with the surrounding multicultural communities.

A useful model that allows for the integration of many of these critical variables is the Ecological Model developed by Bronfenbrenner and enhanced by others. According to this model, we try to understand or evaluate a student (the microsystem) in the context of his/her mesosystems (immediate family, extended family, friends, network), macrosystems (culture or subculture), and exosystems (social structures).

This model places the diverse learner, school staff, and parents/community in an ecological context, which then allows both for a broader understanding of the critical issues affecting students from diverse backgrounds and the development of relevant service and educational models. These educational models need to be highly sensitive to the particular community and social contexts of which the diverse learners and school staff are members.

For the diverse learner and the school staff, the ability to conceptualize and integrate culture and issues of diversity within a developmental perspective is also crucial, given the changes in developmental tasks at each life stage and the various ways that these "tasks" are expressed and resolved within various cultural groups.

Relevant to the diverse learner in schools, these issues must be integrated within the specialized early intervention programs offered to children with developmental issues. Early intervention services are an extremely important part of the total, life-stage conceptualization for low income, diverse learners because such learners are more vulnerable to developmental concerns.

Through the development of multicultural competencies within the areas of awareness, knowledge, and skills, the probability increases of psychologists using assessment and treatment strategies that meet the needs of a wide range of culturally diverse groups. The need for flexible and culturally sensitive assessment techniques has continued to be stressed by many in the field.

Examinations of the critical features in assessment should include the sociocultural context of the diverse learner and his family, the sociocultural background of the examiner, such as issues of awareness of biases and stereotypes, and the selection of appropriate testing, interview, and survey instruments.

All of these measures enhance the possibility of more relevant and culturally sensitive assessments. Furthermore, the consideration of issues related to language and its complexities is another major factor in providing relevant and meaningful assessments.

The need for changes in the conceptualization of children's abilities and how skills are assessed, particularly with diverse learners, has also led to strategies that focus on problem-solving abilities.

Maker, Nielson, and Rogers described the need for change in assessments within a diverse school settings, including the assessments of students who are to be considered "gifted." The authors presented various assessment programs that rely on Gardner's theory of multiple intelligences and they provided an analysis of problem-solving strategies for individual children.

These procedures stress the process of problem solving and they offer an examination of each child's pattern of multiple intelligences in an attempt to get away from the more traditional and, at times, rigid analyses based on formal intelligence and skills testing. Likewise, the model of Maker, Nielson, and Rogers has great implications for the assessment of children of all levels and children from diverse backgrounds. Their model allows for individual analyses of children's particular problem-solving style and strengths, which are then encouraged, while areas for remediation are addressed.

Intervention strategies also need to incorporate the critical issues of culture and social context. Works on specific cultural groups, such as Lock on interventions with African American youth, Jackson on counseling youth of Arab Ancestry, Thomason on counseling Native American clients, Zapata on working with Latinos, and Yagi & Oh on interventions with Asian American youth, provide valuable guidelines on working with specific populations and serve to increase awareness of the specific cultural factors relevant to that particular cultural group.

Awareness of, and the ability to assess, specific factors such as acculturation, language proficiency (including guidelines on the use of translators), and sociocultural history, further enhances the provision of culturally affirming treatment strategies. The need to deal with diverse groups must also include work with gay and lesbian youth and youth with disabilities, particularly as we proceed with educational inclusion models which are further enhancing the diversity presented within school systems.

With the changing composition of today's student population, the need to provide educational programs that address the complex issues related to multiculturalism and diversity is becoming more and more evident.

Schools and educators must begin to develop curriculums that integrate awareness, knowledge, and skills within educational materials. It is critical that diversity and multiculturalism not be conceived as being accomplished by adding a course, a lecture, or a one-day "multicultural fair."

A total curriculum transformation needs to take place where the critical issues of diversity and multiculturalism are integrated into all aspects of students' academic achievement, social skills development, and relationship with the community at large.

An example of such an attempt is the work of one of the authors who developed a psycho-educational course to help students increase their self-awareness, acceptance and appreciation of the self and others, and communication skills. The course was tried in two multicultural schools and in one school comprised mainly of minority children. The response from the students and teachers of both regular and special education classrooms was positive. They noticed the nurturing climate developed through the course.

The opportunity for children to begin to integrate into their lives issues related to multiculturalism and diversity is vital to the development of acceptance and respect for others from diverse backgrounds.

Along with traditional educational models that present historical and social information about people from diverse backgrounds, the creation of models that stress the development of awareness and cultural sensitivity skills needs to take place. Under this general category of enhancing multicultural awareness and respect for diversity is the critical need for confronting issues of racism and prejudice.

Another major component in working with diverse learners is that of establishing "authentic" relationships with parents and the community. This is a critical element of any effort directed towards increasing multicultural understanding and the development of a truly pluralistic school and community environment.

To become actively involved in school is hard for immigrant parents who are not familiar with American school systems. Workshops on American schools including structure, rules, services, and the rights and responsibilities of parents and children are found to be helpful, even empowering, to these parents.

The need for direct work with parents and communities has been stressed by Atkinson and Juntunen: "... school personnel must function as a school-home-community liaison, as an interface between school and home, school and community, and home and community". Casas & Furlong, writing with regards to Hispanic parents, but offering ideas clearly applicable to other multicultural groups, stress the advocacy role of school counselors both to "...increase parent participation and facilitate the increase empowerment..." of parents and the community. This is a critical role that needs to be taken on not just by school counselors, but by all school staff working with diverse learners in an increasingly multicultural environment.

In short, learners from diverse multicultural groups, children with disabilities, and gay and lesbian youth will continue to present challenges to schools and those providing educational and support services.

The development of educational curriculums that enhance awareness, knowledge, and skills for students is vital if schools are to provide culturally relevant, respectful, and affirming teaching environments. To that end, the development of culturally sensitive assessment and intervention strategies, multicultural consultation, and professional training needs to take place. Structured along the lines of awareness, knowledge, and skills development, such actions will enhance diversity within the school environment.

The diverse student and community can be conceptualized as a wonderful and exciting element of the world we live in, and not as a hindrance to the educational process. The authentic involvement of parents as active and empowered members of the school community will link school staff with the diverse learner, further increasing and affirming cultural diversity within our school settings

Valuing Diversity in the Multicultural Classroom

Educators of children and adults are increasingly aware that learners within a classroom represent a complex array of personal experiences, values, and intentions that can inform curriculum development and classroom instruction. In adult English as a second language (ESL) and family ESL literacy classrooms, learners' ways of understanding and acting in the world may differ radically from those of the mainstream population.

Educators respect and honor their learners' "ways of knowing" when they create and work from curricula that emerge from issues of importance to them. However, too often teachers let their learners' knowledge and views of the world slip by unnoticed.

When learners' ways of understanding the world are not heard and accepted, everyone loses—the learners, who bring this knowledge with them to schools; the parents, who want to pass on cultural traditions but find themselves fighting both the school information and their children's perceptions of the value of their own cultural beliefs; and the teachers, who could be opening new worlds of exploration to children and themselves while providing a bridge between the culture of the school and the culture of the home.

Multi Directional Learning

In effective family ESL literacy programs—where literacy needs of children and their parents are addressed through instruction in English, native language literacy, cross-cultural development, self-esteem, family learning, and home school relations diverse ways of knowing are explored and valued. In these programs, it is especially important that learning be multi- directional: Children, parents, and teachers all learn from one another as they share their experiences.

For example, some family literacy projects use elders' storytelling as a basis for lessons. Other projects encourage children to discuss and value their cultural traditions and family routines.

A teacher in a literacy program for immigrant parents and children in a rural area along the Rio Grande River in Texas used information about his learners' worlds and ways of knowing in a lesson he developed on Halloween in the United States. He provided materials and assistance in making costumes, and he compared the origins and cultural traditions of the U.S. holiday with the Day of the Dead holiday traditions in Mexico and Central America.

Elementary school educators and researchers have done much to inform the field about the importance of valuing families' ways of knowing. One research study shows that classroom practice can be "developed, transformed, and enriched" when researchers and teachers who have received training in interviewing techniques visit minority student households to discover the "historically developed and accumulated strategies (skills, abilities, ideas, practices) or bodies of knowledge that are essential to a household's functioning and well-being".

In participatory adult ESL programs, teachers conduct informal research in the classroom itself using dialogue journals, family trees, life journeys, class newspapers, and speaking and writing assignments from learners' photos. Designed to elicit issues and concerns of importance to learners, these activities also serve to uncover learners' ways of knowing the world. One example of such an activity comes from a program for American Indian parents in Minnesota.

Learners demonstrate the richness of their alternative knowledge by comparing parenting styles and family values of Indian parents to those of mainstream culture. Below is an excerpt from a list of differences they developed.

In short, in adult ESL and ESL family literacy programs, teachers can provide cultural and linguistic bridges to connect the worlds of the home and the classroom by recognizing, honoring, and building on students' ways of looking at and understanding the world and by building curricula and classroom learning around this knowledge. As educators learn to value and build on learners' ways of knowing, learners will in turn value and benefit from the education experience of the classroom.

Multicultural Career Education and Development

The implications fof cultural diversity constitute one of the most critical issues facing the United States today. Census data show rapid increases in nonwhite populations, a vast reserve of human potential that makes a multicultural focus imperative for career education and development.

Wurzel defines multicultural perspective as a critical and reflective understanding of oneself and others in historical and cultural contexts, an awareness of both differences and human similarities. For career educators and counselors, it means infusing practice with an awareness of their own personal and cultural background and experiences as well as those of their students or clients.

Self-concept and identity are crucial to career development. Cultural values and beliefs have great influence on the formation of self-concept; therefore, effective career development must take culture into account.

The purpose of multicultural career education and development is to foster positive self-concepts and career choices regardless of cultural background, encourage understanding of the contributions of all cultural groups, and develop effective intercultural communication skills.

World view—the attitudes, values, opinions, and beliefs with which a person perceives the world—is influenced by cultural heritage and life experiences. Locke and Parker explain how different combinations of Locus of Control (LC) and Locus of Responsibility (LR) affect the formation of world view. Four combinations are as follows:

(1) Internal LC-Internal LR—feelings of high personal control and personal attributions of success or failure;

(2) External LC-Internal LR—acceptance of the dominant culture's definition of self-responsibility;

(3) External LC-External LR—feelings of a lack of both control and responsibility; and

(4) Internal LC-External LR—belief in individual efficacy but perceptions of external barriers to action.

The category that corresponds with an individual's world view derives from his/her cultural background as well as the historical, social, and economic experience of that cultural group. This is the context in which students will attempt to act on their career choices.

One of the dangers of multiculturalism is thinking that all members of a group share identical characteristics. However, cultural awareness must begin with understanding of such differences as world view, bearing in mind that people are a complex product of gender, ethnicity, and individuality.

Another dimension of difference is nonverbal communication styles. Interpretations of words, gestures, spatial and temporal relationships, and touch can vary among groups. Other values and perspectives on which groups may differ are as follows: cause and effect, holistic versus linear thinking, competition versus harmony, long- versus short-term goals, view of the teacher or counselor as authority or facilitator, collectivism versus individualism, degree of tolerance for ambiguity, assertiveness versus restraint, and authoritarian versus democratic family structures.

Intercultural communication means the ability to approximate another person's meanings, without necessarily agreeing with them. A culturally effective career educator has a wide repertoire of skills to interpret the world views and communication styles of students and to select the best strategies and techniques to help them.

An El Paso, Texas, project provides an example. Hispanic females have high dropout rates and the lowest college attendance rate of any ethnic population. The alienation of many Latinas from school stems from lack of role models and counseling, stereotypes in curriculum, and low teacher expectations.

Mothers are a strong influence, but many mothers have low educational levels and lower expectations for their daughters. The Mother-Daughter Program jointly operated by the University of Texas, the YWCA, and El Paso School District builds on the strong maternal influence.

Sixth-grade girls and their mothers participate in a program designed to acquaint them with careers and college, raise aspirations, introduce them to Hispanic female role models, and help mothers to be role models. The program targets sixth-graders because it is felt that the pre-high school period is a critical time before girls conform to cultural norms and restrict their own options.

Program activities include campus tours, career day, community service projects, awards ceremonies, and summer camp, a 2-day immersion in campus life. An important factor in the program's success is respect for the participants' language (using bilingual materials) and cultural traits.

Techniques for Career Development

A key to effective career education and development for diverse groups is the sensitivity and awareness of educators and counselors. Locke and Parker describe the cross-cultural awareness continuum, which educators and counselors can use to gauge their growth in intercultural competence, a lifelong, ongoing process. The levels of the continuum are as follows:

— Self-awareness

— Awareness of one's own culture

— Awareness of racism, sexism, and poverty

— Awareness of individual differences

— Awareness of other cultures

— Awareness of diversity

— Career education skills/techniques

Culturally skilled career counselors or educators are aware of their own ethnicity and personal prejudices, have knowledge and understanding of culturally diverse groups, and have knowledge of culturally relevant strategies, skills, materials, and resources.

Examples of a secondary and a postsecondary program illustrate ways of integrating multicultural techniques. The Iowa Department of Public Instruction's approach to secondary multicultural career education begins with the premise that students must see themselves reflected in the curriculum and must see the potential for themselves in various careers. The curriculum has five parts:

(1) self-concept (including race, sex, national origin, and physical condition);

(2) understanding of the world of work;

(3) understanding of the contributions of all groups to society;

(4) commonalities of the human race, uniqueness of individuals and cultural groups; and

(5) interpersonal and intergroup communication.

The Iowa curriculum includes a self-evaluation checklist to assess the following aspects of schools and programs:

— Diverse role models on staff

— Diverse student enrollments across courses and curricula

— Multicultural, nonsexist content integrated into curriculum philosophy, goals, objectives, and evaluation

— Instructional materials representative of cultural diversity and gender

— Culturally aware teaching strategies, behavior, and attitudes

Case Western Reserve University's Minority Career Awareness Program addresses three factors considered important in minority career development: friendly atmosphere, leadership opportunities, and a sense of success.

The program features the student-run Careers Unlimited Corporation (CUC), which sponsors workshops that provide interaction with minority professionals. The CUC simulates workplace situations, enabling students to develop and test leadership abilities in a supportive environment, receive feedback on interpersonal skills, and learn about organizational dynamics.

The following strategies synthesize from a number of sources some approaches to multicultural career education/development:

— Teachers and counselors should establish a climate of acceptance, have high expectations for student achievement, and foster positive self-concepts and cultural identity.

— A cultural group should not be thought of as homogeneous. For example, Asians are composed of many different subgroups. Native American differences appear among tribes, in urban and rural environments, and intergenerationally. Teachers should strive for a balanced view of students as individuals and group members.

— Curriculum materials should be representative of all groups in a wide range of careers.

— Bilingualism should be valued and students' language and culture incorporated in instruction. Students should be helped to learn the difference between feelings of superiority and pride in one's heritage. Reflective teaching practices and sharing of the teacher's own ethnicity and background can foster a sense of community.

— Differences in communication styles, learning styles, and decision-making styles should be assessed and appropriate teaching and counseling methods selected.

Issues in Multicultural Approach

Although a goal of career development is empowering people to change their lives, a focus solely on individual competence ignores the effects of external forces.

Teachers and counselors are encouraged to be advocates for students by recognizing problems that are systemic rather than individual. Acting as change agents, they can seek commitment from administrators for a multicultural perspective, examine institutional practices and the values they represent, and question the assumed universality of theories, methods, and instruments used in career development.

Lee and Richardson recognize the potential of counselors as systemic change agents but identify some concerns about an overbroad definition of multiculturalism and the potential for a new kind of racism by overemphasis on differences. They present the following considerations for a multicultural approach:

— The importance of a group's history, the way its perspective is derived from exclusion from power

— The level of ethnic identity and acculturation

— Influence of family, sex role socialization, and religion

— The way a group has been named or labeled

— Some groups' traditional mistrust of counseling and education as tools of social control

Locke and Parker conclude that system commitment to meaningful career education, a belief that students can learn and want to learn, and educators and counselors who value the worth and dignity of all students are the keys to successful multicultural career development.

Multicultural Counseling

Multiculturalism has been defined as the fourth force in psychology, one which complements the psychodynamic, behavioral and humanistic explanations of human behavior.

Pedersen defined multiculturalism as "a wide range of multiple groups without grading, comparing, or ranking them as better or worse than one another and without denying the very distinct and complementary or even contradictory perspectives that each group brings with it".

Regardless of how one defines the term or the degree to which the concept is restricted or broadened in a particular context, multiculturalism encompasses a world of complex detail. There are four dimensions of cultures. These dimensions are:

— *Power distance*—the extent to which a culture accepts that power in institutions and organizations is distributed unequally.

— *Uncertainty avoidance*—the extent to which members of a culture feel threatened by uncertain or ambiguous situations.

— *Individualism*—a social framework in which people are supposed to take care of themselves and of their immediate families only. Collectivism refers to a social framework in which people distinguish between in-groups and out-groups, expecting their in-group to look after them, and in exchange for that owe loyalty to it.

— *Masculinity/Femininity*—the extent to which the dominant values within a culture are assertiveness, money and things, caring for others, quality of life, and people.

A number of generic counselor characteristics are necessary, but not sufficient, for those who engage in multicultural counseling. To be effective, a counselor must be able to:

- Express respect for the client in a manner that is felt, understood, accepted, and appreciated by the client. Respect may be communicated either verbally or nonverbally with voice quality or eye contact.

- Feel and express empathy for culturally different clients. This involves being able to place oneself in the place of the other, to understand the point of view of the other.
- Personalize his/her observations. This means that the counselor recognizes that his/her observations, knowledge, or perceptions are "right" or "true" only for him/herself and that they do not generalize to the client.
- Withhold judgment and remain objective until one has enough information and an understanding of the world of the client.
- Tolerate ambiguity. This refers to the ability to react to new, different, and at times, unpredictable situations with little visible discomfort or irritation.
- Have patience and perseverance when unable to get things done immediately.

Counselors bring with them their own degree of effectiveness with these generic characteristics. They also bring with them their cultural manifestations as well as their unique personal, social and psychological background. These factors interact with the cultural and personal factors brought by the client.

The interaction of these two sets of factors must be explored along with other counseling-related considerations for each client who comes for counseling. The effective counselor is one who can adapt the counseling models, theories, or techniques to the unique individual needs of each client. This skill requires that the counselor be able to see the client as both an individual and as a member of a particular cultural group.

Multicultural counseling requires the recognition of:

(1) the importance of racial/ethnic group membership on the socialization of the client;

(2) the importance of and the uniqueness of the individual;

(3) the presence of and place of values in the counseling process; and

(4) the uniqueness of learning styles, vocational goals, and life purposes of clients, within the context of principles of democratic social justice.

The Multicultural Awareness Continuum was designed to illustrate the areas of awareness through which a counselor must go in the process of counseling a culturally different client. The continuum is linear and the process is developmental, best understood as a lifelong process.

— *Self-awareness.* The first level through which counselors must pass is self-awareness. Self-understanding is a necessary condition before one begins the process of understanding others. Both intrapersonal and interpersonal dynamics must be considered as important components in the projection of beliefs, attitudes, opinions, and values. The examination of one's own thoughts and feelings allows the counselor a better understanding of the cultural "baggage" he or she brings to the situation.

— *Awareness of one's own culture.* Counselors bring cultural baggage to the counseling situation; baggage that may cause certain things to be taken for granted or create expectations about behaviors and manners. For example, consider your own name and the meaning associated with it. Ask yourself the cultural significance of your name. Could your name have some historical significance to cultures other than the culture of your origin? There may be some relationship between your name and the order of your birth. There may have been a special ceremony conducted when you were named.

The naming process of a child is but one of the many examples of how cultural influences are evident and varied. Language is specific to one's cultural group whether formal, informal, verbal, or nonverbal. Language determines the cultural networks in which an individual participates and contributes specific values to the culture.

— *Awareness of racism, sexism, and poverty*. Racism, sexism, and poverty are all aspects of a culture that must be understood from the perspective of how one views their effect both upon oneself and upon others. The words themselves are obviously powerful terms and frequently evoke some defensiveness. Even when racism and sexism are denied as a part of one's personal belief system, one must recognize that he/she never-the-less exists as a part of the larger culture. Even when the anguish of poverty is not felt personally, the counselor must come to grips with his or her own beliefs regarding financially less fortunate people.

Exploration of the issues of racism, sexism, and poverty may be facilitated by a "systems" approach. Such an exploration may lead to examination of the differences between individual behaviors and organizational behaviors, or what might be called the difference between personal prejudice and institutional prejudice. The influence of organizational prejudice can be seen in the attitudes and beliefs of the system in which the counselor works.

Similarly, the awareness that frequently church memberships exist along racial lines, or that some social organizations restrict their membership to one sex, should help counselors come to grips with the organizational prejudice which they may be supporting solely on the basis of participation in a particular organization.

— *Awareness of individual differences*. One of the greatest pitfalls of the novice counselor is to overgeneralize things learned about a specific culture as therefore applicable to all members of the culture. A single thread of commonality is often presumed to exist as interwoven among the group simply because it is observed in one or a few member(s) of the culture. On the contrary, cultural group membership does not require one to sacrifice individualism or uniqueness.

Total belief in individualism fails to take into account the "collective family-community" relationship which exists in many cultural groups. A real danger lies in the possibility that counselors may unwittingly discount cultural influences and subconsciously believe they understand the culturally different when, in fact, they view others from their own culture's point of view. In practice, what is put forth as a belief in individualism can become a disregard for any culturally specific behaviors that influence client behaviors. In sum, counselors must be aware of individual differences and come to believe in the uniqueness of the individual before moving to the level of awareness of other cultures.

— *Awareness of other cultures.* The four previously discussed levels of the continuum provide the background and foundation necessary for counselors to explore the varied dynamics of other cultural groups. Most cross-cultural emphasis is currently placed upon African Americans, Native Americans, Mexican Americans or Hispanics, and Asian Americans. Language is of great significance and uniqueness to each of these cultural groups, rendering standard English less than complete in communication of ideas. It is necessary for counselors to be sensitive to words which are unique to a particular culture as well as body language and other nonverbal behaviors to which cultural significance is attached.

— *Awareness of diversity.* The culture of the United States has often been referred to as a "melting pot." This characterization suggests that people came to the United States from many different countries and blended into one new culture. Thus, old world practices were altered, discarded, or maintained within the context of the new culture. For the most part, many cultural groups did not fully participate in the melting pot process.

— *Skills/Techniques.* The final level on the continuum is to implement what has been learned about working with culturally different groups and add specific techniques to the repertoire of counseling skills. Before a counselor can effectively work with clients of diverse cultural heritage, he or she must have developed general competence as a counselor.

Passage through the awareness continuum constitutes professional growth and will contribute to an increase in overall counseling effectiveness, but goes much further than that.

Counselors must be aware of learning theory and how theory relates to the development of psychological-cultural factors. Counselors must understand the relationship between theory and counselors' strategies or practices. Most importantly, counselors must have developed a sense of worth in their own cultures before attaining competence in counseling the culturally different.

Multicultural Issues in Supervision

Perhaps two of the most important changes within counseling and counselor education in the past twenty years have been (a) recognition of the need for a multicultural perspective in all aspects of counseling and education and (b) the evolution of supervision models and practices. Recently, these changes culminated in two sets of competency and standards statements that will most certainly guide counselor preparation and evaluation of counselor practice.

The Association for Multicultural Counseling and Development (AMCD) approved a document outlining multicultural counseling competencies and standards and the Association for Counselor Education and Supervision (ACES), adopted comprehensive standards for eleven aspects of counseling supervision.

Now counselors are recognizing the need to consider multicultural issues in supervision and methods of multicultural supervision. The multicultural perspective will become essential as we move into the twenty-first century. It is projected that by the year 2010 twelve of our most populous states, containing about half of the nation's young people, will have significant minority populations. Thus, the supervision triad of client, counselor, and supervisor will most likely contain persons of differing racial-ethnic backgrounds who are confronting problems and concerns in a diverse social environment.

The supervisor is responsible for assuring that multicultural issues receive attention in supervision. Generally, whenever the client is a minority group member, and sometimes when either the supervisee or supervisor is a minority person, supervisors will recognize the relevance of addressing cultural concerns. However, all counseling and supervision contacts have cultural, racial-ethnic aspects which shape core assumptions, attitudes, and values of the persons involved and which may enhance or impede counselor effectiveness.

Logical extensions of this view of multicultural supervision are models that advocate supervision as a method to assist multicultural counselor development. These models propose that supervisees move in stages from minimal racial-ethnic awareness, to awareness of discrepancies between cultures and within self, and then to development of a multicultural identity.

The supervisor's role is to promote supervisee growth by challenging cultural assumptions, encouraging emotional expression, and validating conflict of attitudes and values. These multicultural models lack empirical support, but seem to integrate well with developmental models of supervision and direct the supervisor to assess the multicultural awareness level of each supervisee.

A number of supervision techniques have been proposed to insure that the cultural dimension is addressed, though none have research support. Planned discussion of culture and the culture of counseling; exploration of supervisee and supervisor cultural backgrounds; required use of videotape; modeling by the supervisor; inclusion of cultural considerations on all intake, case management, and other written supervision reports; and experiential exercises are methods that can be used in individual and group supervision.

All supervision is some form of multicultural supervision, supervisors will need to be proficient in the multicultural competencies. All supervisors-in-training should work with supervisees from racial-ethnic groups other than their own and receive supervision of multicultural supervision. Likewise, experienced supervisors will need to seek continuing education, consultation, and focused supervision of supervision with a multicultural emphasis to meet gaps in experience and education.

CHAPTER 5

Education: The Social Cohesion

The education system in the region generally has been overly concerned with academic performance of students and has been paying very little attention to their emotional needs. It is true that parents have an important responsibility to raise emotionally healthy children. The reality, however, is that many parents, as a result of their own inadequate socialization, do not themselves have the skills to perform this critical role. Indeed, many of them as a result of this inadequacy inflict enormous emotional damage on their young charges. The education system, therefore, has a key role to play in fostering emotionally healthy children. The focus can no longer be exclusively be on academic concerns. A holistic approach must be adopted in the education of young persons in the region if the system is to contribute to the promotion of social cohesion and the reduction of levels of societal violence.

A holistic approach to delivery of education implies that the role of the teacher has to be perceived very differently from what has been traditionally accepted. The essence of the role of a teacher in the Caribbean in the twenty-first century must be to assist in the moulding of well-adjusted young persons who:

— Are able to love themselves;
— Are emotionally secure;
— Are full of self confidence;
— Take full responsibility for their actions;
— Trust their own thinking;
— Respect self and others;
— Respect the views of others even when different from their own;
— Respect persons of different cultures;
— Respect and treat with dignity persons with physical and other disabilities;
— Acquire good writing, speaking, listening and numerate skills;
— Acquire competent information-seeking skills;
— Acquire sound problem-solving skills and good critical thinking skills;
— Additionally, young persons need to be put in touch with their innate spirituality.

Commentary on desired personal attributes

The issue of responsible sexual behaviour, for example, not included here, is of paramount importance in today's world. However, the elements highlighted constitute an indispensable core for moulding the personalities of socially and emotionally well-adjusted young persons who, embodied with these characteristics, will be centres of inner calm and who will not only promote social cohesion, but will be predisposed to achieve personal success in whatever field of endeavour they choose to pursue. Loving yourself implies accepting yourself as you are, warts included, while taking active measures to change those personal characteristics that you deem in need of being changed.

One who does not love self is incapable of loving anyone else. Self-hate is the antithesis of self-love. It is intimately linked with personal insecurity and lack of self-confidence and is usually the cumulative result of systematic mistreatment in early childhood. Someone who is overwhelmed with self-hate is capable of doing an enormous amount of societal damage, including the perpetration of overt forms of violence. Learning to disagree with someone else's point of view and yet respect it as valid is the basis for nurturing a culture of tolerance in society. This also provides a basis for respecting and accepting persons from different cultures.

Teaching young persons to trust their own thinking is a big challenge for parents and the educational authorities. It is so easy instead to teach them to trust the thinking of the authority figure. But this is a trap because it serves to erode self-reliance, making it easy for such persons to be led astray by strong personalities who indulge in antisocial behaviour. A key point highlighted here is that the spark for the promotion of social cohesion has to be ignited by the individual through feeling at ease and comfortable with the self.

Powerlessness as a deterrent to social cohesion

When a person or group of persons feels powerless, it is sometimes in relation to a perception of others having power over them. When young people, particularly young males, feel a sense of powerlessness and alienation, they are likely to promote disharmony in society. If what transpires in the classroom contributes to making the students feel a sense of powerlessness, this is likely be counterproductive to fostering social cohesion and a culture of non-violence. Conversely, if the classroom atmosphere is one of partnership between teacher and students, rather than a power relationship in which the teacher is seen as the authoritarian figure, this is likely to facilitate the development of self-confidence and social responsibility among the students. It ought to be self-evident that the use of corporal punishment as a sanction in the school system is quite inappropriate, because it is simply impossible to promote a culture of non-violence through the use of violence.

The teacher as counsellor in the classroom

In many countries of the region, guidance counsellors are attached to schools. One of the main aspects of their function is to interact with students who manifest behavioural problems. Their function is usually conducted outside of the normal classroom activities where the students interact with teachers teaching the various subject disciplines. Although the 'fire fighting' role of guidance counsellors is important, what is even more critical is that teachers function as counsellors in their normal classroom interaction with their students.

Functioning as counsellor in the classroom simply means that the teacher adopts as a norm a nurturing, pupil-enhancing posture where every child is treated with full respect, is listened to attentively and is perceived as valuable and capable of learning. It is such an environment that is most conducive to young students learning to love and respect themselves and others. It is not necessarily easy for teachers to function in this nurturing mode where students are given constant attention and encouragement. Often their working reality is one of overcrowded classrooms, with children exhibiting all kinds of disruptive behaviour. Additionally, the teachers themselves, like all other normal adults, are saddled with their own emotional 'baggage', in the form of their unresolved emotional issues. It is this 'baggage' which will tend to manifest itself as inappropriate reactions to classroom situations. It is quite a challenge for the teacher to see the student as separate and distinct from his/her disruptive behaviour.

Curruculum Implications

Traditionally, the curriculum has been perceived as the elements of the course content of the particular academic subject being taught. It appears, however, that increasingly, it is being recognized that everything that is relevant to classroom dynamics can be a legitimate concern for the curriculum. This development is fortunate because it is important that the elements or attributes cited for the moulding of socially and emotionally well-adjusted young persons be made explicit in school curricula irrespective of the academic subject matter being taught.

Values education should be made an important content component of curricula in primary and secondary schools. Activities such as the Peace and Love in Schools (PALS) programme, spearheaded in Jamaica, could be evaluated to identify what generic elements can be adopted in curricula throughout the region. In addition, an initiative such as the Health and Family Life Education programme that has been endorsed by Ministries of Education throughout the English-speaking Caribbean could be very useful in communicating important values to young persons.

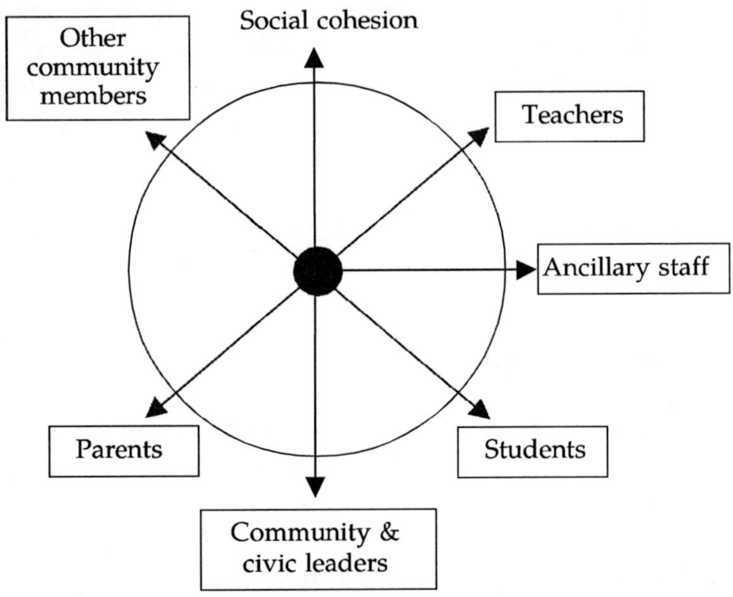

Figure 1: Involving all stakeholders in curriculum implementation

If, however, we were to rely primarily on the course content of material to be imparted to students in primary and secondary schools throughout the region to promote social cohesion and a culture of non-violence among the youth, we would be missing the mark. What is of even greater importance in the socialization of these students during classroom hours is the quality of the teacher/ student interaction, independent of subject matter being taught. Whether they are teaching mathematics or social studies, teachers in primary and secondary schools of the region will find that, when they adopt an approach which aims to nurture and encourage students, not only will they contribute effectively to producing emotionally healthy young adults, but management of their classrooms will become considerably less problematic.

Changing the Culture of the Classroom

There are many conscientious and dedicated teachers throughout schools in the Caribbean, but their ability to create, on an ongoing basis in their classrooms, a nurturing, valuing environment will very much depend on their own early socialization and how successful they have been in releasing emotional hurts encountered in their early youth. It will be recalled that culture was defined simply as usual or normative ways of being, doing and relating. It is clear that, for the objectives being sought, the entire culture of the classroom has to be one in which students are encouraged to believe in and develop their abilities.

The Changing the Culture of the Classroom programme, which has been led by UNESCO/CARNEID, has been eloquently described by Colleen Winter-Brathwaite in EFA in the Caribbean: assessment 2000. However, some additional remarks seem relevant in the current context. In a Changing the Culture of the Classroom training workshop that was conducted with teachers from a junior secondary school in Trinidad and Tobago, the teachers reacted with great surprise when that there are no problem students. One teacher interjected 'If there are no problem students, you have to be implying that there are problem teachers.' The basic point that was being established is that the student must be seen as a distinct entity, not to be identified with his/her behaviour, however inappropriate that behaviour might be. When the student is seen by the teacher as separate from the behaviour it is then possible for the student to be helped by that teacher.

In these experiential training workshops, the teachers learn specific skills for classroom management. At the same time, they explore themes such as: early distress experiences and the natural recovery process; the essence of the role of the teacher; the concept of flexible intelligence; internalized oppression and its impact on behaviour; limited categories of new adult hurt; the concept of restimulation of early distress experiences; acknowledgement and appreciation of student efforts as a nurturing tool; appropriate and inappropriate sanctions; use and misuse of the syllabus; the undesirable use of fear as a control mechanism; the challenge of maintaining discipline in the classroom; empowerment of the teacher for optimum effectiveness.

Although the topic of this presentation has implications for young and old in every Caribbean society, the emphasis in this discussion has been on education in the regular school system, in particular at the primary and secondary levels. The education systems in the region, as well as individual teachers, have to redefine their role. This should essentially be seen as the moulding of socially and emotionally well-adjusted young persons who are equipped with both a well-defined set of personal attributes and a predetermined range of aptitudes and skills.

This reorientation of focus away from the short-sighted academic emphasis will more than likely lead in the medium term to societies which are more socially cohesive and in which there is much less violence because young people will emerge from the school system with a healthier self-concept. This change of emphasis to a more holistic model of education has profound implications both for the development of school curricula, and for teacher orientation and retraining. As much emphasis has to be placed on 'how' things are done in the classroom as on 'what'. Thus, in the design of curricula as much attention needs to be placed on the strategies for implementing course content as on the course content itself.

Education for Social Cohesion

We have to begin by specifying why social cohesion may be considered to be one of the objectives of education. This, in turn, leads us to identify different approaches to the subject. Some, descended from the functionalist sociological tradition and starting from a neutral stance towards values, postulate forms of social cohesion which are aimed at sustaining and reproducing a given social order and alleviating conflicts. Others, following a critical tradition with clear libertarian leanings, identify and analyse the forms of social cohesion that appear in a historically determined society and become morally committed to achieving forms of social cohesion that are more just and humane. It is not a matter of obtaining just any form of social cohesion, but one that produces the best results in terms of liberty, equality and solidarity among the members of society.

In the field of education, those theories exerted a powerful influence over the educational policies that were developed in the last century in the countries of the region. In a nutshell, it might be said that the former approach influenced the spiritualist and positivist belief that education systems should be part of the process of constituting and consolidating nation states. The second approach, on the other hand, was more related to critical education and so-called 'popular education' movements, and has been behind many of the educational reforms developed in recent decades. Although the effect of these reforms on general practices cannot yet be evaluated, it may be observed from their theoretical constructions that their strength resides in the critical aspects of social diagnosis. On the other hand, that strength is not apparent in terms of a moral commitment, when it comes to proposing forms of social cohesion and effective ways of achieving it. In relation to the critical approach, the criticism of traditional teaching methods has invalidated many of the methods that have proved effective in traditional education. One example is the reluctance in such approaches to offer practical ethical education, on the assumption that it is enough for the latter to be implicit in scientific training and in educational practice, or their tendency to restrict specific ethical training to the formation of moral judgement.

Another example, related to more practical teaching methods, is the negative attitude to storytelling. These resources of traditional education, which have proved useful in the past for building shared feelings and expressing emotions and values, have been depreciated on the grounds that they are subject to the risk of ideological abuse. Because of these and other drawbacks, eclectic positions have emerged in most of the curriculum reforms in Latin America, with elements being taken from both approaches under different labels, such as humanist, systemic, holistic or integrationist. Our own work has been part of this search for improvement, which led to the process of curriculum reform developed in Argentina between 1995 and 1999.

An effort was made to recover social criticism and some of the tools of traditional education. The aim has been to direct educational processes towards the achievement of forms of social cohesion which maximize the potential of all the members of the educational community, with particular attention for the potential of the most underprivileged. In order to give a brief overview of this approach, we may look in turn at its main elements, namely learning contents, educational subjects and learning processes, in relation to traditional education. Traditional education never pretended to inquire into the nature and dynamic of social and political life; on the contrary, it presents the forms of life as something already given. Its analysis of such forms amounts to mere consideration of technical matters of organization. Value considerations remain external to the system concerned. For instance, learning about democracy or economic systems in this case means learning about how social life is organized through legislation. It does not matter whether that legislation complies with ethical principles or not.

The knowledge acquired must merely ensure that actions correspond to the prescribed rules, without enquiring too much either into the underlying basis of the rules or into the way they are assumed. Thus, the sphere of practice is reduced to the technical problem of getting to know predetermined rules and abiding by them. As the rules do not need to be 'critically assumed', changes occurring in the legal framework will produce not reactions, but merely adjustments to resolve once again the technical problem of adaptation.

Approaches aimed at improvement, on the other hand, should emphasize the ethical principles which support democracy as a form of government and a lifestyle, namely liberty, justice and solidarity. It entails a critical approach to these principles, which begins in the early stages of education with the recognition that they are needed for social coexistence, moving gradually towards an assimilation of the principles as independently as possible in the higher levels of education. The effort of subjecting these principles to philosophical criticism of their foundation, scope and application in itself implies an opportunity to learn these contents. In view of the concern for social cohesion in our countries, the principle of justice deserves special mention among contents that need to be learned. This is because social justice is one of the weightiest concerns of our societies. There can be no real social cohesion in unjust societies.

Equal opportunities for accessing knowledge and participating in dialogue should therefore be recognized as necessary conditions for social cohesion. Once this is recognized, it will provide a basis for a feeling of solidarity with the most underprivileged and the starting point for a practice directed towards change. This objective therefore constitutes the keynote of our proposal and should become the focus of educational processes aimed at achieving greater social cohesion in the countries of the region.

Having a knowledge of social processes and organizations also means knowing them as legal organizations based on those ethical principles, i.e. standard setting entities socially and historically established to guarantee a certain social cohesion and to administer conflicts. The critical approach helps to understand the perfectibility of rules established in relation to given circumstances and subject to stated ethical principles. Right from the early stages of education, students can learn and understand the meaning and scope of such rules.

Gradually they can learn to relate to them, by observing them, criticizing them and participating in their construction. This is why it is also important to impart a sense of the historic awareness of the circumstances in which the rules used to organize social life are constructed and developed. In the present context, for instance, for any analysis of democracies, families or social working relations, it is essential to refer to institutional crises, the search for new models of representation and participation, the nation-state identity crises brought about by globalization, changing methods of production, etc. If students are able to find some beacons within the uncertainty of change, this will give them a better understanding of the dynamic quality of concepts such as 'democracy', 'family' and 'community'. Hence when learning the modes of organization of social life, it is important not to lose sight of the fact that these forms of organization are 'historically situated'.

Developing a Learning Community

With regard to those who are the subjects of education, the central notion that prevails in traditional education is the notion of the individual, through references to individual achievements, individual obligations, individual responsibilities and individual rights. On the other hand, educating for social cohesion makes it necessary to consider the learning subject as a learning community. Social cohesion implies coexistence; therefore the minimum subject cannot be the individual, as a being aware of standards/norms, but rather the 'cohabitants', i.e. the 'learning community'.

This working approach raises the need for educational contents which are relevant for dealing with the challenges facing the countries of our region, namely a sense of belonging and solidarity. The school, in its traditional socializing function, provides a scenario of coexistence that can bring together traditions and communities of different origins. In this scenario, students and teachers undergo the daily experience of building a collective identity that allows for their differences. The outcome of this experience will then to a great extent determine the future integration of the citizen in the public life of the local, regional or national community.

Preparedness for participation and public responsibility does not manifest itself spontaneously on departure from school. It requires a considerable effort of learning which begins when at the very outset of education the subject learns to appreciate the meaning of the word 'us'. It later culminates in the knowledge and appreciation that individual differences and conflicts resulting from those differences are not an obstacle, but are part of the process whereby this collective identity is constructed. These differences and conflicts can therefore offer opportunities to enrich the collective identity insofar as they are duly treated as a means of learning the ethical principles that are being pursued. Hence, the importance of changing the way students are considered in our countries, which are faced with the challenges of redefining identities in the context of globalization and of the changing relationships between the state, society and the market. The socializing function of the school, which was often in the past suspected of complicity with the prevailing ruling systems, must now be recovered, in line with this perspective, as offering the possibility of rebuilding a public awareness in the face of the divisive and individualizing tendencies which prevail under the hegemony of the logic of the marketplace. This also implies a change in the attitude of teachers, who can be active players in constructing this communal, transforming subjectivity, to the extent that they become aware that they too are cohabitants. Learning for social cohesion therefore requires a 'classroom atmosphere', where the ethical principles that constitute democratic life emerge as ideals governing concrete practices. It requires an opening of the school to the community. Converting the physical space of schools into an open centre for cultural activities in the community has proved to be an effective means of tackling problems that seriously affect social cohesion, such as juvenile violence and drug addiction.

Learning Processes

With regard to learning processes, traditional education was centred on a knowledge of the modes of organisation of social life as laid down by the law, without much concern for the ways such laws were assumed. By contrast, the central notion underlying education for social cohesion is that of praxis, understood more in the sense of acting than as mere technical doing. Praxis is action charged with meaning and values. This also raises the need for a comprehensive consideration of actors. Traditional education was geared to focus only on the cognitive capacity of students.

Today, affective and practical aspects must also be included. It is not a matter only of knowing how a particular community is ordered and what it values, but of knowing whether that order or that set of values can stand up to rational criticism, and of checking whether the reasons put forward to defend it are sufficiently convincing to want to act in accordance with those rules and values, and consequently to act.

For example, in our society we might consider that co-operation is an essential value for social cohesion and that, as such, it is something that our educational system should support. So ethical training should not only provide the necessary tools to learn that co-operation is socially valuable, but it should also provide an opportunity for the student to analyse critically the reasons why co-operation is said to be good, while at the same time undertaking to ensure that the student wants to and knows how to co-operate effectively. To put it in simple terms: it is not a matter only of knowing that it is good, but also of knowing why it is good and in addition wanting to do good and knowing how to do it.

In this way the school could provide a forum for reflection and action which could help detect and criticize existing values and moral standards. This in turn would enable students to adopt behaviours and habits consistent with those principles and standards. It would also allow students to develop capacities for judgement and action that conform to the ethical principles. It is generally recognized that confronting problem situations is a very useful teaching tool for training moral judgement. When such situations involve the modes of organization and related practices, the tool becomes even more useful. Knowledge and dialogue are essential elements, which developed in suitable conditions combine to facilitate cautious decision-making. A knowledge of codes, procedures, processes and the institutions involved is needed to identify the best solution to problems. Rational dialogue, in which reasons are put forward and well-founded arguments are exchanged, provides the opportunity to arrive at agreements and to settle conflicts peacefully.

Whence the importance that both students and teachers should acquire basic abilities for dialogue and discussion and should prefer consensus as an ideal way of resolving conflicts. Among dialogue and communication strategies, special emphasis should be placed on those aimed at the nonviolent resolution of conflicts. Persuasion, negotiation, mediation and arbitration are commonly used strategies in democratic societies which can and should be learned in schools.

The practical approach which is proposed means changing the definition of students as agents in order to consider them as actors. Agents are people who represent and/or reproduce an external discourse. In the traditional approach, education trains agents to reproduce social, political and economic discourses which are alien to their own interests and realities. The critical approach proposes instead to train actors, that is, subjects who are able to choose and therefore able to construct their own courses of action and the social and political systems in which they participate. Such actors, while being part of political, legal and economic systems, are in no way predetermined by them, but thanks to their margin of liberty and to the extent of their possibilities, may become creative transformers of those systems.

Another trait to be developed in actors is a strategic capacity for action. This implies an ability to assess the effectiveness and efficiency of different resources or courses of action in order to attain specific targets. With regard to social cohesion in particular, it is best to be able to experiment with different forms of collaboration, co-operation and association in order to be able to appreciate the various possibilities and limitations of individual and collective actions. School plays a fundamental role to the extent that it offers students considerable opportunities for internalizing the values and procedures of democratic life by exercising institutional participation, which includes knowing how to participate, to dialogue, to petition and to claim rights, to resolve conflicts, to elect and be elected, to be represented and to represent, to build standards and fulfil obligations, etc. This enables them to face the complexity of exercising democracy, to understand the dynamic of its processes better and to assess its scope and limitations as a form of social coexistence and political organization. Actions of solidarity on the part of the school towards the community, stimulated and planned from within the school with a clear pedagogic purpose, have proved to be extremely effective educational strategies.

Combined with the learning of the ethical principles underlying these practices, they can lead to a noticeable improvement in the motivation of students by helping them to understand the significance and relevance of other learning contents. In the light of all the foregoing arguments, it may be concluded that no education for social cohesion is possible unless it is practised in schools, both in the classrooms and at the managerial and organizational level, and projected on the surrounding communities.

Chapter 6

Educational Inequalities in Infoage

The term 'globalisation' has become quite widespread, even in the popular media, there are confused and often conflicting definitions and conceptions of the phenomenon. In order for this concept to maintain any analytical usefulness, it must be unpacked, carefully defined and examined for its impact on society, the economy, and the world system. At its most organic and fundamental level, globalisation is about the monumental structural changes occurring in the processes of production and distribution in the global economy.

These structural changes are responses by many global enterprises that confront tremendous pressures and fantastic opportunities presented by the increased application and integration of advanced information and communications technologies (ICTs) into their core business processes (e.g. R&D, manufacturing, testing, back-office operations, marketing, distribution). Through the application of information and communications technologies, enterprises have the ability to diminish the impact of space, time and distance.

Global companies can break apart business functions that were previously thought to be best collocated (i.e. within the same geographic area), and spread them across the globe in a globally disarticulated labour and production process. This aspect of globalisation requires the existence and development of an advanced information and communications infrastructure, based on a network of networks of telecommunications, broadcasting, computers, and content providers. This network of networks—a Global Information Infrastructure—currently does not exist. Such a GII should be a robust, global, broadband, high-capacity network, most likely based on fibre optic cable networks.

The internet and World Wide Web currently come closest to meeting these requirements. However, as sociologists Manuel Castells argues, "the Integrated Broadband Networks (IBN) envisioned in the 1990s could surpass substantially the revolutionary 1970s proposals for an Integrated Services Digital Network (ISDS)".

At a more conjunctural and secondary level, globalisation is affecting all of the social, political and economic structures and processes that emerge from this global restructuring. One critical issue that emerges from all of these restructuring processes is the central role of knowledge, education and learning for the success of the Global Information Society (GIS) and global information economy. Knowledge is becoming an increasingly important factor of production.

Education in a Global Information Society

There is an underlying focus on the impact of globalisation on knowledge, education and learning and the promises and challenges of the Global Information Infrastructure—Global Information Society (GII-GIS) to meet the increasing needs and demands of the world's citizens.

The global political economy is experiencing massive changes and fundamental internal and external restructuring. It has gone from a dynamic system which produced, for some, a "golden age" of capitalism in the 1950s to a system that is facing a global crisis. The current crisis is being foisted upon the world by a fundamental change in the underlying structures of production and distribution within the global economy.

As a result of this restructuring a new development model is emerging. Since the 1950s, the dominant model for techno-economic development has been the Fordist—Taylorist development model. Fordism—Taylorism rested upon three major pillars. The first pillar was the factory system and mass production. The second pillar was the application of scientific management. And finally, the third pillar was the moving assembly line. These practices enabled the Fordist—Taylorist development model to "more efficiently harness physical labour from huge masses of relatively unskilled shop-floor workers." This Fordist—Taylorist model was only fully implemented in the advanced industrialised countries which has tremendous implications for the developing countries within this current period of global economic restructuring.

The global system of production and distribution is now progressing from this Fordist—Taylorist development model to one based upon what Richard Kenney and Martin Florida call Innovation-Mediated Production. Innovation-Mediated Production, challenges significantly the Fordist—Taylorist development model and is based upon the blurring of the distinctions between mental and physical labour and the increase in the application of knowledge to the production process itself. This change is so significant that it represents a fundamental shift, for much of the world, in the underlying technological and economic paradigm (techno-economic paradigm) of industrial organization.

On the one hand, the highly industrialised countries of the world, as represented by the Organisation for Economic Cooperation and Development (OECD), are adapting to this techno-economic paradigm shift through various strategies, and high-levels of public and private sector cooperation. On the other hand, the developing countries are facing a tremendous tidal wave of changes, opportunities and challenges in this new era of globalisation and economic restructuring, which in many cases is overwhelming capacity.

The knowledge intensive nature of this development model—Innovation-Mediated production—requires firms to invest heavily in research and development (R&D), not as a luxury or solely to gain competitive advantage, but to survive.

In some countries, this research system has been developed into a National System of Innovation, which harnesses the resources of the public sector, private sector, academic sector and non-governmental organizations. One area that has garnered a huge share of R&D expenditure in the developed countries has been optoelectronics. Optoelectronics represents the fusion of photonics technologies (using photons as the delivery mechanism) with microelectronics (using electrons as the delivery mechanisms) "to attain greater efficiency in data processing and transmission than electronics can achieve by itself."

The application of optoelectronics has produced radical new developments in information and communications technologies. This increased focus on optoelectronics is "drastically revolutionizing the communication system and [is] widely expected to form the next generation of information-based technologies." These new technologies have given us the Internet, World Wide Web, Integrated Systems Digital Networks (ISDN), Asynchronous Transfer Mode (ATM), Electronic Data Interchange (EDI), and a host of other technologies that have fuelled the Information Revolution.

In addition, the increased application of digitization techniques blurs the distinctions between telecommunications, computers, broadcasting and other high-technology sectors. Analysts have developed a concept to describe the blurring of lines between "once separate industries into an integrated digital marketplace."

The Optoelectronics Revolution, amongst many other components, facilitates what Jeffrey Henderson calls the "Global Option." By applying these new information and communications technologies, firms are now able to promote a globally disarticulated production and distribution process. This means that the various components of the production and distribution process—R&D, manufacturing, testing, information management, advertising, and marketing—need not be in the same geographic location. In fact, these various components can be, and are often, spread out on continents around the world.

For example, R&D can take place on one continent, manufacturing on several different ones, testing on another continent, and information management on still another. The advertising and marketing of these products can take place on a global scale with niche marketing tactics—even if the public relations firm is located in a small remote country. All of these activities are currently taking place, they are increasing, and they are proceeding at the speed of light. Henderson calls this the "World Factory" phenomenon.

Global corporations, especially those competing in the converging high-technology industries, have increasingly expressed the tendency to utilize the new Innovation-Mediated development model and to explore the Global Option. The incessant technological development of the new techno-economic paradigm, the convergence of telecommunications, computers, and broadcasting, along with the increased pressures for global deregulation, liberalization and market-access have radically altered the global political economy and have undermined the existing the international telecommunications regime.

International regime theory, as developed in the social sciences, attempts to address the so-called "anarchy problematique." This intellectual construction addresses the ways in which "sovereign and equal" nation-states, operating in an anarchic world system in which there is no juridical or de jure authority over them attempt to address issues which are by their very nature transnational. Regime theory suggests that there are various mechanisms within the world system that facilitate the development of specific norms, principles, and values relating to the issue area and the mechanisms to enforce those norms, principles and values.

Telecommunications is one of the issue areas around which one of the oldest and most successful international regimes has emerged. The International Telecommunication Union (ITU), has served as the centrepiece of this regime, with tremendous benefits flowing to national PTTs. Several social, economic, political and technological factors are converging to undermine this regime.

Globalisation and the Information Revolution present increasing difficulties for national states as they attempt to make choices about how to respond and allocate their scarce resources to confront this challenge. This challenge is particularly acute for African countries that are being bombarded with multiple "options" as to what actions and strategies are appropriate for their particular countries.

Knowledge as a factor of production within this new information-intensive economy, is gaining in importance in the era of globalisation. The education and learning paradigm around the world is under increasing pressure to better meet the demands of this new knowledge and information-intensive global economy. As these developments lurch forward, it is extremely important that social scientists, national-governments, non-governmental, international and regional organisations, and the private sector, attempt to understand the impact of globalisation on the global political economy and on local realities.

The existing literature on globalization and the Information Revolution is to a large degree theoretical and overly speculative. There is a need for a clear theorization of globalization and the transformation occurring in the global economy which is grounded in an empirical analysis of local realities, including the knowledge, education and learning requirements for the information age.

Given the increasing economic globalisation and restructuring in the world political and economic systems, and the requirements for knowledge and information within that system, educational needs (in terms of structure, function, curriculum and approach) at all levels, especially at the tertiary level, have changed. These educational requirements for the workforce of the future are extremely important. However, the systems developed for informal learning, specifically for adult learners to engage in life-long learning, are important as well.

There are significant contrasts between knowledge, education and learning. "Education is generally seen as a formal process of instruction, based on a theory of teaching, to impart formal knowledge (to one or more students)." However, the process of learning can occur, with or without formal institutional education. "Knowledge accumulation and the accumulation of skills for using ICTs will occur increasingly outside the traditional institutions of formal education. Learning in the workplace, and through collaborations that sometimes span the global and at other times involve tightly nit local communities with similar interests, will become more commonplace."

However, knowledge should not be limited to a select few. As the store of knowledge expands throughout the world, all of the world's people should have as much access as possible. However, the "formal institutions of education that exist today, and even many of these in the planning stages in developing countries, are becoming less relevant to the requirements of emergent 'knowledge societies'."

Mansell and Wehn argue that these countries must actively reshape their educational systems in ways that are "consistent with their national priorities." However, these national priorities must now take into consideration the fundamental changes occurring in the underlying structures of the global economy and new strategies for achieving competitive national advantage.

The role of knowledge within the economy is leading to a whole range of new industries and new developments in biotechnology, new materials science, informatics, computer science, etc. Within this new framework for knowledge, education and learning, there are at least ten components that should be included and or enhanced.

Some of the challenges for knowledge, education and learning in this period will be ability for today's learners to be more familiar and comfortable with abstract concepts and uncertain situations. Much of the academic environment today, presents students with ready-made problems and then asks them to solve them. The reality of the rapid-fire global economy, based on information and knowledge is that problems are rarely that clearly defined. It requires those seeking valuable employment to seek out problems, gather the necessary information, and make decisions and choices based on complex uncertain realities.

Much of the education and learning environment today is divided into very rigid academic disciplines, focused on discrete units of research. However, the emerging Information Society and global economy requires a holistic understanding of systems thinking, including the world system and business ecosystems. Thus interdisciplinary research approaches are seen as critical to achieving a more comprehensive understanding the complex reality currently facing the world system.

Symbols are highly abstracted manifestations of some concrete form of reality. Highly productive employment in today's economy will require the learner to constantly manipulate symbols, such as political, legal and business terms and concepts, and digital money. These "symbolic analysts," as Robert Reich calls them, are in high demand.

In the past, academic practitioners often saw themselves as wise "sages on the stage" delivering data, information, knowledge and wisdom to the eagerly awaiting students, whose minds were empty vessels waiting to be filled. However, if that reality were ever true, the world's store of knowledge is increasing at such a monumental rate, that no single person can hope to adequately convey as comprehensive an understanding of a subject as is possible, or as could be absorbed by most students. The Global Information Infrastructure Commission (GIIC), an international, independent, non-governmental private sector organisation argues that:

The globalization of the economy and its concomitant demands on the workforce requires a different education that enhances the ability of learners to access, assess, adopt, and apply knowledge, to think independently to exercise appropriate judgment and to collaborate with others to make sense of new situations. The objective of education is no longer simply to convey a body of knowledge, but to teach how to learn, problem-solve and synthesize the old with the new.

There are a range of new technologies and new techniques engendered by the Information Revolution that allow for the production of new knowledge and the dissemination of data, information and knowledge. Some of these technologies include the Internet, World Wide Web, CD-ROM, and printed, audio, video and other electronic media forms. These new technologies allow for academic practitioners to move from being "sages on the stage" into the role of the "guide on the side" and assist students in gaining the skills and abilities required to acquire and utilise knowledge contained in various forms around the world.

The kinds of industries emerging in the age of globalisation—such as biotechnology, new materials science, human genetics, advanced computing, artificial intelligence, and human/computer interfaces—demand that employees remain highly trained in science and technology. Research and development is a critical component, and many countries are trying to develop National Systems of Innovation (NSIs) that attempt to harness the combined resources of its academic institutions with the research enterprises within the public and private sectors. In these countries, universities will have to quickly adapt to the needs and provide a key component of such national systems.

The Fordist-Taylorist development model made strict separations between mental and physical labour. However, the new innovation-mediated paradigm requires a much more holistic approach to the business enterprise and valorizes the intellectual contributions of all employees. In fact, most observers would find it very difficult to make concrete distinctions between many Information Age-oriented manufacturing facilities and computer laboratories.

Working in teams requires students to develop skills in group dynamics, compromise, debate, persuasion, organisation, leadership and management skills. Most academic institutions and programmes are set up to do the opposite, to force students to think only of themselves and their own personal development, perhaps with some very limited group work. Not only should students learn to work in teams; but also they should learn to work in global networked virtual teams. These global virtual teams are being used increasingly in industry and international organisations for R&D activities. Chris Dede argues that "Computer-supported collaborative learning (CSCL) enhances team performance through tools for communicating each person's ideas, structuring group dialogue and decision making, recording the rationales for choices, and facilitating collective activities."

As command and control systems disintegrate around the world, academic institutions must become less rigid and more flexible in their attempt to meet the varied needs of learners and the global economy. This includes variety in time, place, approach and curriculum offerings. As new issues and industries emerge within the global economy, academic course offerings should be adapted to reflect these new knowledge, education and learning requirements.

Using advanced information and communications technologies, a new system of knowledge, education and learning should apply a wide range of synchronous and asynchronous activities that aid the professor and student in breaking the boundaries of space and time. Synchronous activities can include real-time lectures (featuring audio, presentations, web sites, and even video), quizzes and group discussions; all of which can occur with the instructor being at the same location or even a different location from the learner. Asynchronous activities can include archived lectures (in audio and video), and other archived course material that can be accessed at nearly anytime, anyplace.

To meet the knowledge, education and learning challenges and opportunities of the Information Age, the GIIC argues:

It is not, however, sufficient anymore to raise the efficiency of the existing systems of education and improve the quality of their components. Even the best of them have served another set of demands for another age.

Graduates of these systems, to varying degrees, now find themselves deficient in knowledge as well as cognitive skills that are necessary for the increasingly sophisticated living environment and for the ever-evolving labour market. More importantly, knowledge based businesses often complain that graduates lack the capacity to learn new skills and assimilate new knowledge.

To meet these challenges and to reap the benefits of the opportunities presented by globalisation, active responses should occur within the public and private sectors at national, regional and international levels. At a national level, these requirements for knowledge, education and learning should be addressed with policy approaches that:

1) allow as many people as possible to engage in productive healthy forms of employment that enhances their quality of life; and

2) meet the increasing demands of global enterprises operating within the global economy.

Developing countries are behind significantly in the information infrastructure required to generate and disseminate knowledge. One concept that could address these concerns is the emerging vehicle of Multimedia, Multipurpose Community Information Centres (MPCICs or Telecentres). Current research indicates that these centres could serve as effective vehicles for enhancing the knowledge, education and learning opportunities for communities in emerging economies.

Within the private sector, at national levels, there are efforts to strengthen the partnership between the private sector and public sector in the delivery of education and learning. Again, the GIIC argues that there are specific roles for the private sector within this framework, because the educational establishment may not be able to redefine itself sufficiently to meet the requirements of the new information-intensive economy. The Commission sees three critical roles for the private sector in the education sector. The first recommended role for the private sector is the rethinking of education.

The Commission argues that. "Since its success depends to a large extent on the product of the educational system, the private sector should engage in the rethinking of education to meet the demands of the age of globalization and information by providing, systematically, input into the analytical and decision making processes in areas such as strategic shifts, curricula, restructuring, standards, and evaluation."

Collaboration in training for the new economy is a second role recommended by the GIIC for the private sector in education. This recommendation springs from an assumption that the training within private institutions has the following advantages:

1) employers can train workers quickly and place them into positions;

2) training costs are lower;

3) the technology in these enterprises is usually advanced;

4) quick responses to the needs of the marketplace.

Finally, the GIIC suggests that the provision of educational services is a critical role for the private sector in education. It argues that the public sector will be unable to continue bearing the major financial responsibility for the financing and provision of education.

With the escalating demands and the diversification of avenues of dissemination of knowledge, governments will not be able to be the sole providers of education. There will be more opportunities for the private sector to provide educational services with a competitive edge based on efficiency, flexibility, management style, and information technology. The obvious domain is at the secondary and tertiary levels as well as in the fields of skill development and upgrading and lifelong learning.

The GIIC believes that it is in a unique position, "at the intersection between technology and private businesses," to make a positive contribution to promoting these concepts around the world. It suggests the following responses for the GIIC in collaboration with its members and international partners.

— Create and support a forum to connect scientists, information technologists, policy makers, and practitioners for the purpose of rethinking education in the age of globalization and information.

— Support mechanisms for the exchange of ideas and experiences in the use of educational technologies.

— Encourage explorations, experimentation to push the frontiers of the potential of information technologies and communications for more effective learning.

— Engage in the design of pilot "learning communities" that expands the time and space dimensions of education.

— Encourage, and engage in, collaborative schemes for the development of educational curriculum-related software that can be used worldwide to achieve economies of scale and expertise.

— Support the design of information infrastructure that is most appropriate for education and that is cost-effective, implementable and sustainable at large scales.

Whether or not the GIIC engages in these activities, it is clear that at global, regional and national levels, within both the public and private sectors, there is a need for concrete responses in knowledge, education and learning to the challenges and opportunities presented by the age of globalisation. The next section focuses on key examples at each of these levels.

In short, globalization is a very real phenomenon that is transforming the world economic system including nearly all aspects of production, distribution and other business processes. With the emergence of a new development model, particularly in the highly industrialised economies, knowledge and information take on increasing importance. Thus, the era of globalisation has tremendous concomitant implications for knowledge, education and learning. The new system of knowledge, education and learning should include the following ten key components.

— A focus on abstract concepts;

— Uses a holistic, as opposed to linear, approach;

— Enhances the student's ability to manipulate symbols;

— Enhances the student's ability to acquire and utilise knowledge;

— Produces an increased quantity of scientifically and technically trained persons;

— Blurs the distinction between mental and physical labour;

— Encourages students to work in teams;

— Uses virtual teams around the world;

— Is an agile and flexible system; and

— Break the boundaries of space and time.

National inequalities in education

Countries are divided into low-income and high-income groupings, and people into low-income and high-income households. Differences in wealth matter, because they define opportunities for reducing poverty. But differences in wealth reflect deeper inequalities in life-chances, including inequalities in education. As economic activity becomes increasingly knowledge-based, disparities in educational opportunity will play a more important role in determining the distribution of income and poverty.

Global inequalities of educational opportunity are not just a matter of crude differences between North and South. Disparities between developing countries are also marked, with important implications for the distribution of income between developing regions.

Comparisons between regions and countries provide an insight into average performance. But in education, as in other areas, averages conceal differences based on wealth, gender, region, ethnicity, and other factors.

National inequalities in education are often greater than North –South inequalities. Just as the latter reinforce highly unequal patterns of income distribution in the global economy, inequality in the distribution of national opportunities for education enables the wealthy to capture a disproportionately large share of national wealth. These national inequalities cast the global education crisis in a new light.

The crisis is fundamentally a crisis for the poor, since there are only a few countries in which the rich have not achieved universal basic education. The final section uses a disaggregated version of the EPI to capture the extent of inequality across a wide range of dimensions by ranking different regions of the same country.

Contrasts between a typical primary school in Europe or the United States and a similar facility in rural sub-Saharan Africa or South Asia capture some of the dimensions of global inequality in education. In much of the developing world, 'school 'is often a dilapidated mud building with crumbling walls. More than 80 children, many of them undernourished, might be crammed into a classroom, sitting on the floor with scarcely a book, pencil, or notepad to share. Their teachers, most of them untrained, may have second jobs to make ends meet.

Rote-learning will be the order of the day. Water and sanitation facilities are likely to be grossly inadequate. Primary schools in industrialised countries face problems of their own –but they are problems of a different order. Teachers are well trained, class sizes are smaller, paper and pencils will be in plentiful supply. The school will have a library, and probably computers. The walls will be decorated with the work of the children, maps, and other visual aids. Each child will have access to a set of core textbooks. While the national media and parents 'associations may take the view that schools are in a state of perpetual crisis, it is a crisis of a different order than that which prevails in the developing world.

The material contrasts between the education systems of rich and poor countries reflect huge disparities in financing capacity. The problem is not that poor countries spend a smaller share of their national wealth on education than rich countries.

In fact, sub-Saharan Africa spends a larger share of its GDP –around 5.6 er cent – on education than the OECD countries spend, though many countries in the region spend far less than the average. Measured in terms of public effort, Africa has been investing more in primary education than other regions, and also increasing that effort over time.

The problem is that disparities in wealth translate into huge disparities in spending, which in turn produce highly unequal outcomes in terms of public provision for basic education. This is especially true when, as in Africa's case, economic decline reduces the absolute value of any given proportion of GDP invested in education.

Some indication of the financial divide separating education systems in the developed and developing worlds can be provided by a simple profile of expenditure. With one-fifth of the world 's population, the industrialised countries account for more than four-fifths of total public spending on education. At the other extreme, South Asia accounts for almost 25 per cent of the world 's population, but for only Economists typically think about poverty and inequality in terms of income.

On average, the OECD countries spend $4636 per student through public finance for primary and secondary education, compared with $165 per student in developing countries and $49 in sub-Saharan Africa.

To take relative spending in 1980 as the point of comparison, per capita public spending on education in sub-Saharan Africa and South Asia is now 60 per cent lower than average spending in the industrialised world. In Latin America, it is one-third lower. Only East Asia has closed the financing gap in education, although this picture has almost certainly changed in the wake of the financial crisis.

While inefficiencies in public spending contribute to the education gap separating rich and poor countries, differences in national wealth, related in turn to the distribution of global income, are the main determinant of the financing gap.

Demographic factors are reinforcing the effects of differential growth rates and initial income inequalities. In the industrialised countries, the size of the population aged under 15 has contracted by about 6 er cent since

1995, while per capita incomes have grown at more than 2 er cent a year. Spending per pupil has risen significantly as a result, even though the share of GDP allocated to education has been static.

In developing countries, the population aged under 15 has grown by one-third over the same period, while problems of economic stagnation and debt have, in many cases, reduced financing capacity. The importance of demographic trends can hardly be overstated. At any given level of average income and unit cost of schooling, countries with higher rates of population growth will face relatively higher per capita costs in progressing towards education for all.

In the developed countries, children aged 6 –11 typically comprise 5 –8 per cent of total population, and population growth is now zero. In sub-Saharan Africa, the 6 –11 age group typically represents more than 15 per cent of the population, rising to 20 per cent for countries such as Tanzania, Zambia, and Uganda. It is not just that the education budgets of these countries are infinitesimally smaller than those of developed countries, but that these smaller budgets must cover a primary-school population that is three times larger in relative terms.

Financing differences are marked at all levels of education, but the biggest gap is to be found at the primary level. Taking into account only recurrent budgets, per capita spending on primary-school pupils in Nepal and India is about $12, compared with $5130 in the United States.

Annual spending per primary-school pupil in Britain is equivalent to $3553 –around 130 times more than in Zambia. At one level, these simple spending comparisons give an exaggerated picture of the problem. The costs of materials, buildings, and teachers 'salaries are obviously higher in the developed countries, so that the same provision costs more.

At another level, financial comparisons understate the problem. They do not, for instance, capture the high levels of private spending on education in the industrialised countries. In the developing world, millions of households do not own a single book; the consequent restrictions on children 's academic development are obvious.

By contrast, recent research in Britain, the USA, and Australia found that more than 80 per cent of children of primary-school age had 25 or more books at home. This illustrates how private spending capacity widens the already extreme differences in opportunity associated with differences in public spending.

Comparisons of public spending fail to capture another dimension of financial inequality. Pressure on recurrent expenditure in many of the poorest countries means that teachers 'salaries often account for more than 95 per cent of spending –leaving almost nothing for the purchase of teaching materials, or the maintenance of schools.

Non-salary recurrent expenditure at the primary level in much of sub-Saharan Africa is less than $2 per pupil, which explains the generalised lack of textbooks and other teaching materials.

While inequalities in education provision and quality are greatest between developed and developing countries, countries in transition are also facing acute problems. They too are falling further behind the high-income industrialised countries, with a major crisis on the horizon in parts of Eastern Europe and the former Soviet Union. Highly developed education systems are collapsing in the face of declining public investment and falling living standards.

Compulsory and free basic education up to the mid-secondary level, high levels of gender equity, and, especially in the sciences, good standards of learning were among their achievements.

Today, however, the education systems of the region are crumbling in a context of economic stagnation, rising inequality, and declining State provision. In education as in other areas, there is a growing danger that the positive inheritance from the past will be lost in the process of transition to market economies.

Oxfam has witnessed at first hand the collapse of education systems through its work with marginal communities in Armenia, Azerbaijan, and Georgia, the former Soviet republics in the southern Caucasus region. For these communities, the rising direct costs of schooling, such as expenditure on textbooks, meals, transport, and other services that were previously provided free, combined with wider economic pressures, notably declining wages and unemployment, put education out of people's reach.

At the same time, the reduced provision of schooling, especially in areas affected by conflict, and its deteriorating quality are widely perceived as problems. The precise mix of demand and supply factors varies from place to place. But the crisis is real, and it has profound implications for economic recovery and social equity.

The following are among the problems which must be addressed to prevent further decline of the education systems in these transition economies:

— *The erosion of compulsory and free basic education*: Most Central and Eastern European countries have restored enrolment to pre-transition levels. This is not the case in the former Soviet republics, which have witnessed dramatic declines in enrolment both at the primary level and in general secondary education. UNICEF has estimated that as many as one in seven children may now be out of school in Central Asia and the Caucasus. Half a million Russian children aged between 6 and 10 are now missing from each grade in the school system.

— *Rising costs*: The cost to families of educating children has risen dramatically. Budgetary constraints mean that schools are now encouraged to raise their own funds. Parents are meeting a growing share of school budgets and teachers' salaries out of their own pockets. Textbooks, once free, are now being charged for, along with notebooks and pencils. These rising costs come during a period when family incomes have been eroded by declining wages, rising unemployment, and inflation. At the beginning of 1996, the price of a package of basic materials for school in Azerbaijan was about $50. The average monthly wage was only $13.

— *Declining public provision*: For many countries, 'transition' has become a euphemism for a shrinking national economy. In 1997, real GDP in the Caucasus countries was less than 40 per cent of the 1989 level, less than 60 per cent in Russia's case. Economic decline on this scale inevitably diminishes the government's capacity to finance basic services through public revenues. Unfortunately, the problem has been exacerbated by political decisions to reduce the proportion of revenues allocated to basic services, including education.

— *Deteriorating quality of schools and schooling*: Precipitous declines in public spending have taken their toll on school infrastructure and service provision. Buildings and equipment have suffered disproportionately, with many schools in a state of chronic disrepair. One in five of Georgia's schools has been classified unsafe and unfit for occupation. In most of the former Soviet republics, teachers' salaries are now below the poverty line, forcing many to take second jobs. Low teacher morale, like deteriorating school buildings and declining public investment, is a sign of diminishing educational opportunity.

It would be wrong to conclude that the systems of education developed under central planning provided a model of uniform good practice. The quality of education often left much to be desired, with a great emphasis on learning facts by rote, rather than on child-centred development. School-management and teaching practices were generally rigid and authoritarian, with little parental involvement. There were also limits to equity, with rural areas often disadvantaged, and ethnic groups suffering discrimination.

But, while reforms to central planning were urgently needed, responsibility for developing a coherent education policy and for funding equitable access seems to have been abandoned. The transition to a situation in which household income determines access to educational opportunities is inherently inefficient in economic terms.

The fact that this transition is occurring at a time of rapidly rising poverty and social inequality carries grave implications for social equity and cohesion today, and for future prospects of social and economic recovery.

Good-quality primary education provides the foundation on which individuals and countries can progress to develop higher levels of skills and learning. As production becomes increasingly knowledge-intensive, the development of secure livelihoods will require not only universal primary education, but high levels of transition into secondary and higher education. Many developing countries are ill equipped to make the transition.

The combination of low enrolment and low completion rates in much of the developing world means that children spend far less time in education than children in developed countries. On average, a child entering primary school in the developing world can expect to receive eight to nine years of education, compared with the 15 –17 years that can be expected in developed countries. As always, however, the average conceals as much as it reveals:

— 'School-life expectancy 'in sub-Saharan Africa is five to six years. It is less than three years in Burkina Faso, Mali, Niger, and Mozambique.

— In Bangladesh, 'school-life expectancy 'is less than four and a half years for girls and six years for boys.

Even these cases obscure the full extent of the problem. This is because averages capture the aggregate picture for the entire population, but conceal differences between average outcomes and those for the poorest sections of society. In poor households, school-life expectancy is invariably far lower, and the proportion of children not attending school is far higher.

But in many developing countries the wider consequence of poor-quality education and limited progression through the primary-school system is an exceptionally low rate of transition into the secondary-school system.

The 2015 target of universal primary education has focused international concern on the primary-school system, often to the exclusion of secondary-school education. But the quality of secondary provision is of profound importance, for at least three reasons. First, basic education alone is not enough to ensure the adoption of new production methods and diffusion of new technologies, especially those associated with information and communications.

The expansion of secondary schooling is vital for the development of the higher levels of education upon which national prosperity increasingly depends. Effective secondary schooling fosters the development of more flexible and abstract reasoning skills of the type associated with high-growth sectors of manufacturing and service industries, and there is evidence that secondary schooling is positively associated with the development of export production in higher-value-added areas of production.

Second, limited opportunities for progression to secondary education have the effect of reducing demand for primary education. This is because many parents see primary education as a stepping stone to the secondary education that their children need in order to maximise their income-generation and employment opportunities –

a perspective supported by research that indicates high rates of return in secondary education.

Third, success in accelerating progress towards universal primary education will inevitably increase demand for secondary education. At present, many secondary-education systems are unable to absorb even the trickle of students who progress through the primary-education system.

The current state of secondary education poses acute problems. At least 700 million people live in countries with gross enrolment rates of less than 40 per cent, and another one billion in countries with rates in the range of 30 –70 per cent. Enrolment rates in the former group of countries have not increased significantly over the last decade, and only modest advances have been recorded in the latter group.

As in primary education, sub-Saharan Africa poses the greatest challenge. The region accounts for fully two-thirds of the countries with gross enrolment rates at the secondary level of less than 40 per cent, with fewer than one-third of primary-school children progressing to the secondary level. There are 19 countries in the region with gross enrolment rates of less than 20 per cent, with a large group falling far short of this level. This group includes Malawi, Mozambique, Burkina Faso, Chad, and Mali, all of which have enrolment rates of less than 10 per cent, and Tanzania, where the secondary-school enrolment rate of 5 per cent is the lowest in the world.

East Asia, South Asia, and Latin America have closed the gap, but they still remain far behind the industrialised countries. Moreover, there are large gender gaps in secondary education, with girls accounting for a far smaller share of enrolment in South Asia in particular.

This is the inverse of the situation in industrialised countries, where boys are under-represented.

The transition point between primary and secondary schools is at the midpoint in a cumulative cycle of inequality. Limited progression through the secondary system produces a limited transfer into the tertiary system. Only 3 per cent of African children, 8 per cent of South Asian children, and 17 per cent of children in East Asia progress beyond secondary school. With the exception of Latin America, significant gender gaps remain at higher levels of education.

The contrast between developing and industrialised countries is striking. Several OECD countries have a higher rate of enrolment of young women at the tertiary level than sub-Saharan Africa has achieved for girls at the primary level. More than half of the children entering the education systems of the industrialised countries today will progress through secondary school to the tertiary system. As an OECD report puts it, 'once learning is realised on this scale in upper-secondary education, it is hard to resist the demand for tertiary studies'.

At the other extreme, insufficient learning at the primary level in sub-Saharan Africa means that there cannot be a sustained increase in enrolment at the lower-secondary level. Some of the differences are especially stark. While millions of girls in South Asia and Africa never step inside a school, women now account for the majority of tertiary enrolments in most OECD countries.

As the process of globalisation integrates developing countries ever more deeply into a knowledge-based global economy, differences in educational opportunity at the secondary and tertiary levels will increasingly distort the benefits of economic growth in favour of rich countries. Without a sustained expansion of coverage and an improvement in education quality at the primary and secondary levels, developing countries will fall further behind at the tertiary level.

In turn, as tertiary education becomes more important to innovation, economic growth, and employment, the wealth gap and the education gap will create a vicious circle of economic decline and rising global inequality.

The communications revolution arrives in the schools of the industrialised world, there is a grave danger that developing countries will be excluded from new areas of learning. And as information technology is integrated more extensively into production systems, the risk of future marginalisation will intensify. In the industrialised countries, telecommunications technology has already revolutionised education. Technological trends in hardware and software have increased the availability and usefulness of computers for education.

Digitalisation has led to the development of computers with multimedia capacity, presenting text, image, and sound to the user. On the software side,' graphical user interfaces 'have made it possible to control computer functions by pointing at pictures rather than by typing text, and to develop interactive programmes for users. Compact discs have made available a vast range of audio and visual learning devices, considerably reducing the costs of accessing information in the process.

Educationalists increasingly recognise the potential benefits of computers for improving the quality of teaching and learning, and expanding the range of information available to children.

Learning opportunities are being revolutionised in particular by the Internet, a worldwide information highway, with easy access via the World Wide Web. Searching among different websites has been facilitated through simple interface 'navigation 'tools, which enable schools to download documents from other computers. Increased access to user-friendly equipment that enables computers to communicate with each other has created what amounts to a 'virtual 'worldwide library.

Access to computers at school is becoming increasingly widespread in the industrialised countries, starting at the primary and the lower-secondary levels. Growing numbers of children also have access to home computers –although the 'digital divide' between rich and poor households is growing.

In the Netherlands, more than half of all households have personal computers, 15 per cent of which are connected to the Internet. Estimates for the USA place the ratio of computers to children at the primary and secondary levels at 1:6. In the SA, Britain, and Denmark, one-third of 14-year-old science students report using computers.

For those with access to information technologies, there are obvious advantages. Students who are familiar with basic computing will adapt more easily to the profound changes that are happening in labour markets with the spread of information technology. They will benefit from higher incomes and wider employment opportunities, and their countries will benefit from associated gains in productivity and competitiveness.

Failure to close the information-technology gap now opening up between school systems in the rich and poor worlds will inevitably result in increasing income inequalities. But the gap cannot be closed by technology and finance alone.

The problem is that the extension of computer technologies to schools requires substantial financial expenditure for the purchase of equipment and the training of staff.

Governments in the industrialised world have turned to the private sector for assistance. But education authorities in the developing world face enormous financial and technical obstacles in obtaining basic computer equipment, with the result that inequalities in access to information technology will start to increase at a far earlier age.

Much has been written about the scope for extending computerised learning systems to the poorest countries. Unfortunately, much of it is divorced from reality. The emphasis has been on the creation of international funds to transfer education technologies through partnerships between development-assistance programmes and private companies. However, many of the poorest countries lack even the most basic infrastructural requirements.

Most schools in sub-Saharan Africa and South Asia do not have the electricity and the telephone lines needed to use computers and access international web sites, let alone the financial resources to purchase them.

In countries such as Mali and Mozambique, where there are fewer than four telephone lines for every 1000 people, and where per capita student spending at the primary level is less than $1, the prospects for effective use of new education technologies are limited. As the effects of inequalities in access to information technology at the primary and junior-secondary levels feed through into the higher and vocational levels of education, the knowledge gap will inevitably widen.

North –South inequalities in access to the knowledge and skills imparted by education will shape future patterns of income distribution in the global economy. However, developing countries themselves are not a homogeneous group. There are marked inequalities in educational attainment across and within regions. These inequalities will also have a bearing, not just on income distribution and future shares of international trade, but also on prospects for human development. Attempting to capture the extent of educational inequality poses serious methodological problems. Most reporting systems refer to data on enrolment rates, completion rates, literacy standards, and gender-based inequality. But measurements in each of these areas are treated in isolation, which can create a misleading picture of overall performance. Countries that achieve a high level of success in enrolment may perform poorly in terms of completion rates.

Conversely, education systems may achieve high rates of completion for those who enter school, while large sections of the population never actually attend school. The Education Performance Index (EPI) provides a more integrated measure of performance across a wider range of dimensions. We use the EPI to rank more than 100 developing countries on a composite indicator for education. The same countries are then ranked on the basis of income. Some of the results are predictable. The EPI confirms that deprivation in education is closely associated with overall levels of poverty. Those countries that are most desperately in need of education to escape the poverty trap have the weakest human-resource base.

Of more interest are the marked discrepancies between educational attainment and average income. Income differences are an important factor in explaining human-resource differences between countries, but they are not the sole consideration. While low-income countries have lower levels of access to education, many score far higher on the EPI than would be redicted on the basis of national wealth. Conversely, many middle-income countries –especially in Latin America –score far lower. These findings suggest that good public policy in education can overcome the disadvantages associated with low income; and bad public policy will reinforce these disadvantages.

The measurement of educational performance has become a highly politicised activity, especially in the industrialised countries. League tables have been developed to differentiate 'successful 'from 'failing ' schools, but a vigorous debate has ensued over what should be measured, and what weight should be attached to various aspects of performance.

The EPI provides a different type of league table. It brings together in a composite index a range of features of deprivation in educational attainment, to arrive at an aggregate judgement on how countries are performing in relation to each other. There are serious problems in developing a composite index. Education data are scandalously poor in many countries. For the mid-decade review of the World Declaration on Education for All, UNESCO produced detailed data on net enrolment rates, completion, and gender equity for most developing countries. However, many of the enrolment rates are little more than 'guestimates', some of which are out of line with evidence derived from household surveys.

According to the World Bank, reliable net enrolment data exist for only about 70 countries. For all their flaws, and despite problems with the data, composite indicators are useful tools. They help to simplify a complex reality on the basis of something more meaningful than a single indicator. When combined with league tables of income, they can also help to compare the performance of countries at very different levels of average income, highlighting important issues of public policy.

The EPI provides a simple composite indicator by concentrating on three aspects of educational performance: namely, coverage, completion, and gender equity. Each of these indicators has a critical bearing on the 2015 target of universal primary education. The specific measurement criteria used are as follows:

— The net enrolment rate, which captures the proportion of children aged between 6 and 11 who enrol in school. This serves as a proxy for the coverage achieved by the school system.

— The completion rate, or the proportion of students who progress beyond Grade 4.

— Gender equity, expressed in terms of the ratio of female to male enrolment.

The EPI measures the average shortfall from a perfect score across the three elements. The higher the score, the larger the shortfall. Data were compiled for 104 countries, which were then ranked on the basis of their performance in each area. An extreme deprivation line was established, representing a threshold where on average more than one-third of children were out of school, fewer than one-third were completing school, and the gender gap in enrolment exceeded 33 per cent.

Finally, the EPI ranking was set alongside an income ranking, using World Bank data for purchasing-power parity in order to provide some insight into the relationship between education performance and average income levels.

Two preliminary observations must be made about what the EPI is –and what it is not. First, the EPI does not capture a number of important aspects of education performance.

Gender equity in enrolment is an important but limited indicator of gender discrimination in education at school and beyond. It does not capture the consequences of gender-biased teaching material, the low self-esteem associated with low expectations on the part of teachers and parents, or the excessive work burdens imposed on young girls.

The EPI is of similarly limited value in measuring education quality. Completion rates are a proxy, but a weak one. In terms of coverage, gross primary-enrolment rates are more widely available than net enrolment data, but they are much less useful. All enrolment data suffer from the problem that they are only a proxy for school attendance. But the difficulty with the gross enrolment rate is that it automatically increases if grade repetitions rise, giving a misleading indicator of performance.

The achievement of gender equity at very low levels of enrolment, or relatively high rates of enrolment with wide gender gaps, should not be obscured by a simple average figure for ranking purposes. For this reason the EPI uses a weighting system that penalises countries for poor performance in each area, thereby limiting the extent of substitution.

Deprivation in basic education as measured by the EPI is closely associated with income poverty and wider human-development indicators. Of course, correlation is not causation. Income poverty does not simply reflect educational attainment.

Even so, with education increasing in importance as a determinant of income and wider life-chances, the interaction of deprivation in education with other aspects of deprivation will intensify. The danger is that failure to overcome educational inequalities will in turn lead to more intensive patterns of marginalisation, especially in sub-Saharan Africa.

There are some obvious reasons why poor countries experience particular problems in providing basic education opportunities. Low average incomes limit the capacity of governments to finance and deliver schooling –the supply of education. Household demand for education is also linked to average income levels and the incidence of poverty.

Poor households are less likely to be able to afford school fees, and more likely to depend on child labour. The overall relationship between income and educational performance is therefore entirely predictable. But the average relationship obscures a more complex picture. Large numbers of countries are under-performing in relation to their income levels; and others are achieving far more than might be expected. There is, in fact, a vast potential for educational opportunity that is being missed because of bad policy choices.

That potential is illustrated by the contrasting performances of good performers, who have achieved a higher EPI rank than their income rank, and bad performers, who have failed to achieve an EPI ranking commensurate with their average income levels. Comparing EPI and income rankings confirms that, in education as in other areas of human development, some countries have performed better than others in converting economic potential into benefits for people.

The benefits of economic growth and rising income in reducing income poverty and child mortality and raising the average level of educational attainment are well established. However, there are striking deviations from this relationship. These are graphically illustrated by the EPI, which shows that many countries have failed to create educational opportunities commensurate with their national wealth.

Latin America has failed in a spectacular fashion to develop a basic education system with a level of coverage and performance consistent with average income levels. Several countries occupy an EPI ranking far below their income rank, among them Colombia, Guatemala, Venezuela, Argentina, the Dominican Republic, Brazil, and Chile.

The Latin American case demonstrates the benefits of a composite indicator. In contrast to poor performers in sub-Saharan Africa, most countries in Latin America have achieved a high level of enrolment, and gender gaps are generally small. However, dropout rates are so high that the average number of years spent in school by the poor in countries such as Brazil is less than that of the poor in countries at much lower income levels, such as Kenya and Zimbabwe. In the cases of Colombia and Guatemala, high dropout rates are aggravated by substantial gender gaps.

The EPI –income comparison confirms the assessment of the Inter-American Development Bank that, taking regional wealth levels into account, Latin Americans –or, more accurately, poor Latin Americans – suffer the world 's worst public education systems. On average, the region 's workforce has had 5.2 years of schooling. If Latin America 's primary-education system had been as effective as the international average for its income levels, the figure would be more than seven years.

Moreover, the percentage of children who drop out of primary school is twice the level that would be predicted on the basis of average-income comparisons. Under-performance in education is both a cause and a consequence of the extreme levels of income inequality in Latin America. Failure to improve performance at the base of the education system will reinforce these inequalities over time.

In some cases, the gap between EPI ranking and income ranking is of extraordinary dimensions. Among the worst cases are Kuwait, Saudi Arabia, Qatar, and Oman. Kuwait and Saudi Arabia respectively account for the largest and second-largest differentials between EPI ranking and income ranking. The underlying reasons for the discrepancy vary.

In the cases of Kuwait and Saudi Arabia, the central problem is a relatively low net enrolment rate. Completion rates for both countries are high, and the gender gap in enrolment is small.

In Qatar, the gender gap in enrolment is the primary problem. For Latin America and the Middle East, the discrepancy between educational performance and potential raises some important policy questions, notably about public-spending priorities.

Both regions show that relatively high levels of public spending and average income do not provide an automatic passport to reasonable levels of educational attainment. However, it is not only middle-income countries and regions that have failed to convert economic wealth into more widely shared opportunities for basic education. There is a large group of low-income countries that are underachieving in relation to their average income levels.

The countries in sub-Saharan Africa clustered beneath the EPI 'extreme deprivation 'threshold illustrate the point. Thirteen of these countries have an EPI rank lower than their income rank, including the following:

- Angola, which has an EPI rank 31 places below its income rank, demonstrating the devastating consequences of the country 's civil war.
- Senegal and Benin, each of which has an EPI ranking 16 places below its income ranking.
- Côte d 'Ivoire, Mozambique, and Niger, with in each case an EPI ranking 8 –9 places lower than the income ranking.

The UNDP 's Human Development Report has consistently shown that poor countries can 'over-achieve 'in human development in relation to their income levels. The EPI confirms this fact in relation to education. But it also shows that poor countries can massively underachieve, highlighting the damaging consequences of factors such as bad policies, conflict, and an unfavourable external economic environment.

One of the worst underachievers revealed by the EPI is Pakistan. The country occupies 99th position in the EPI league table, or 38 places below its income ranking.

Pakistan has an average income equivalent to three times that in Burkina Faso and four times that in Mali, yet it ranks below both countries. This reflects the combination of exceptionally low enrolment rates, a large –and widening –gender gap, and low completion rates.

In each of these cases, failed government policies have aggravated problems associated with low income, contributing to a significant shortfall in performance. Inadequate financial commitment, poor planning, weak administration, and, above all, failures of political leadership have contributed to missed opportunities for education. These missed opportunities imply high costs for human development.

China has a slightly higher average income than Pakistan, but its citizens are three times as likely to enrol in school and almost twice as likely to complete school. The gender gap in enrolment is six times narrower than in Pakistan.

Zimbabwe has a lower average income than Guatemala, but enrolment and completion rates are far higher. Guatemala has a 30 per cent gender gap in primary-school enrolment, while Zimbabwe has no gender gap at that level.

The EPI captures average educational attainment levels for countries. However, national averages obscure deep structural inequalities in education related to enrolment. Household wealth is the single most important factor associated with these inequalities. The poor systematically underachieve in relation to the non-poor, although wealth gaps take different forms in different countries. They also interact with other sources of inequality, including rural –urban differences, gender disparities, regional factors, and ethnicity.

These inequalities do not exist in isolation, but are overlapping and mutually reinforcing. Transmitted across gener-ations,they shape the distribution of opportunity and perpetuate the wider structures which consign people to poverty and marginalisation.

Most governments in developing countries recognise the principle that education is a fundamental human right. Many enshrine that right in constitutional provisions.In practice, however, the right to education is universally enjoyed by the rich, but not by the poor.

In education, as in other areas of social development, wealth matters. Differences in income shape opportunities for education, which in turn shape future patterns of wealth distribution.

There are three broad regional patterns emerge for poor households:

— low enrolment and high dropout rates in much of sub-Saharan Africa (but especially West Africa);

— low enrolment and a less marked dropout rate as far as Grade 5, followed by a sharp increase thereafter in South Asia;

— high enrolment and high dropout rates in Latin America.

The case of sub-Saharan Africa demonstrates how high levels of poverty produce particularly intensive forms of deprivation, starting at enrolment. In Senegal, the enrolment rate for children from the richest 20 per cent of households is more than double that for the 20 per cent. Once in school, children from the wealthy households are four times more likely to complete Grade 1 and five times more likely to reach Grade 5.

In Mali, four out of five children from poor households do not progress beyond the first grade of primary school. Only 2 per cent complete primary school –less than ten per cent of the national primary-school completion rate. Although wealth gaps are widest in West Africa, they are significant across a wide range of countries. In Zambia, for instance, enrolment rates for the richest households are more than one-third higher than for the poorest households.

In South Asia, as in Africa, the proportion of 15 –19 year-olds from poor households who have not completed Grade 1 is very high. Almost half fail to progress beyond this stage. Thereafter, retention in school is much higher than in Africa until Grade 5, when dropout rates increase.

In India and Pakistan, children from the wealthiest 20 per cent of households have almost achieved universal primary enrolment, while less than half of those from the poorest households enrol. Thereafter the wealth gap widens slowly until Grade 5, when it becomes a chasm.

Only 2 per cent of children from the poorest households in Pakistan complete Grade 9, compared with 60 per cent of children from wealthy households. The Indian wealth gap is narrower, but still exceptionally large. Children from wealthy households are around six times more likely to complete Grade 9.

One of the advantages of disaggregated data is that they provide a clearer insight into where the main shortfalls exist in relation to the target of universal primary education. In India, there is a 38 per cent shortfall from universal completion of Grade 5. But only 4 per cent is attributable to children from the richest 20 per cent of households. Almost two-thirds of the primary-school education deficit is attributable to children from the poorest households, which underlines the need for education policy to be integrated into broader anti-poverty strategies.

The Latin American case differs from those of sub-Saharan Africa and South Asia. The pattern here is one of high initial enrolment, followed by a widening wealth gap to Grade 5 and beyond. The education gap is both created by the enormous wealth differences in Latin America and helps to sustain them.

In Brazil, the initial enrolment rate for the poor is similar to that for the wealthy. But whereas four out of every five children from the richest households complete primary school, only 15 per cent of poor households do so. In some countries, wealth gaps in education reach remarkable dimensions. Completion rates for Grade 9 are some thirty times higher for children from wealthy households in Guatemala than for children from poor households.

One of the most striking findings to emerge from household survey data in Latin America is that the level of attainment among children from poor households is not only lower than in East Asia, which politicians in the region typically use as a point of comparison: by Grade 5 it is lower than in sub-Saharan Africa countries such as Zambia and Zimbabwe. Once again, data disaggregation helps to identify the main deficits in relation to the achievement of universal primary education. In Brazil, Peru, and Bolivia, poor children dropping out account for more than 90 per cent of the shortfall in primary-school completion.

Striking as they are, average differences between rich and poor households understate the full extent of the wealth gap in education. Differences in the median grade completed by children in differing wealth rankings reveal even wider disparities. The median represents the middle point in the survey data, and thus avoids some of the problems associated with compiling simple averages. It can be used to compare attainment levels in terms of average years of education across a range of wealth groups.

There are significant differences across all regions. In India, Pakistan, Senegal, Burkina Faso, Côte d 'Ivoire, and Mali, the median grade completed by children from poor households is zero, because fewer than half finished at least one year of schooling. In Africa and Latin America, the median wealth gap typically translates into a situation where children from poor households spend 4 – 7 years less in education than children from wealthier households. The wealth gap in India and Pakistan amounts to 9 –10 years.

It is not only highly unequal countries that suffer from wide wealth gaps in education. Vietnam has one of the world 's most equal patterns of income distribution, but the net enrolment rate for children from the poorest quintile is 10 per cent lower than for the top quintile at the increase the coverage of education provision, while at the same time reducing dropout rates among poor children.

In Latin America, improving the physical availability of schools and the accessibility to all social classes is less of a problem than retaining the children from poor households after they have enrolled. But in all regions, the closure of wealth gaps in education and an increased emphasis on equity are the starting point for accelerated progress towards the goal of education for all.

In developing countries, men living in rural areas are twice as likely to be illiterate as those living in urban areas. Differences between rural and urban women are only slightly less extreme. Such disparities reflect differences in access to basic education.

Limited educational opportunities in rural areas are caused by a combination of factors, ranging from the administrative cost and difficulty of providing services to more remote areas with scattered populations, to the unwillingness of teachers to live in isolated regions, and to demands for child labour. Public-spending priorities that concentrate resources on urban areas add to the problems of rural people.

Overcoming wealth gaps in education is of profound importance to the achievement of the 2015 human-development targets. Bringing the average number of years spent in school by poor children up to the level of their wealthier counterparts would raise the average incomes of poor households, and produce more equitable patterns of income distribution.

Both outcomes would contribute to the halving of extreme income poverty. Similarly, increasing the average number of years spent in school by girls from poor households would help to reduce child-death rates.

Different regions face different challenges if the wealth gap is to be closed. In sub-Saharan Africa and South Asia, the pressing need is to it across generations. Schools in poor rural areas are less accessible, less well equipped, and less able to provide an education of reasonable quality. For instance, 50 per cent of the rural poor live more than 10km from a school, compared with 10 per cent of urban poor households.

Rural schools have fewer qualified teachers and lower completion rates. As a result, the rural poor, who might be expected to reap some of the most significant human-development benefits of education, have the most restricted opportunities. Inequalities in educational opportunity restrict the ability of rural Zambians to work their way out of poverty.

Education can act as a great leveller, but all too often it serves to reinforce disadvantage. Even in countries marked by poor levels of overall attainment, rural populations are frequently left far behind. Only 3 per cent of pupils attending rural primary school in Tanzania proceed to secondary school, compared with 10 per cent of their urban counterparts. One reason for the discrepancy is that only 17 per cent of rural school pupils pass their primary-school leaving exam, compared with 29 per cent in urban areas.

In South Asia, rural –urban disparities are particularly marked, interacting with gender differences. The province of Sindh in Pakistan demonstrates the interaction in a particularly powerful fashion. For a young girl living in rural Sindh, her chance of going to school is half that of a young girl in urban Sindh; and she is twice as likely to leave before completing school.

Inequalities in education between men and women extend across a wide range of dimensions, including enrolment, completion, and the quality of teaching. Cultural, social, and economic factors combine to place young girls and women at a serious disadvantage that starts at school and extends into adulthood. The facts of gender discrimination speak for themselves:

- Women are 60 per cent more likely than men to be illiterate.

- There are 42 million fewer girls in primary school than boys.
- Gender gaps in enrolment have not narrowed significantly, even at the primary level. In South Asia, the net enrolment rate for girls is 20 per cent lower than for boys; in sub-Saharan Africa and the Middle East, it is 10 per cent lower.
- There are 12 countries in sub-Saharan Africa where the gender gap in enrolment exceeds 20 per cent.
- An average six-year-old girl in South Asia can expect to spend about six years in school –three years less than an average six-year-old boy. Even where progress has been made towards improving equity in enrolment, disadvantages in other areas often remain intact.

For instance, India has closed the gender gap in primary-school enrolment by 10 per cent since 1980, albeit to 22 per cent, which is still exceptionally high. Less success has been achieved in reducing the dropout rate for girls.

Gender disparities cannot be considered in isolation. They interact strongly with inequalities linked to household wealth and rural –urban differences. In almost all cases, poverty reinforces gender inequity, so that girls born into poor households face far more restricted opportunities for education than girls born into wealthy households.

In India, nine out of every ten girls from the richest quintile of households are in school, compared with fewer than half for the poorest two quintiles. This wealth-related gender gap widens over the duration of the school career. More than 80 per cent of girls from the wealthiest households complete Grade 8 –almost the same percentage as for boys from the same household. In the poorest households, only one in ten girls completes Grade 8 –and boys are three times more likely to reach this level than girls.

In many countries, wealth gaps aggravate already extreme inequalities between girls and boys. For instance, Nepal has one of lowest ratios of girls 'to boys 'enrolment in the world, and rich and poor families alike are less likely to send girls to school. But in poor families, the enrolment rate for girls is one-third of that for boys. Raising the average incomes of poor households would, in this case, almost certainly reduce gender-based inequity.

Rural –urban differences magnify gender differences almost as much as household wealth does. In Pakistan, completion rates for primary school are twice as high in urban areas as in rural areas. But in rural areas the completion rate for boys is three times higher than for girls, while in urban areas it is only 50 per cent higher. Clearly, cultural, social, and economic factors associated with life in rural areas and with rural poverty exercise a powerful influence.

Important as wealth is, it cannot be taken as axiomatic that any increase in household income will improve gender equity. The relationship between income disparity and the gender gap is complex. Where the education of girls is regarded by parents as being of less value than the education of boys, economic pressures associated with low income will have adverse consequences for gender equity.

Girls are likely to be the last into school and the first out when times are hard. However, this tendency is not universal.

Evidence from sub-Saharan Africa suggests that, while boys are often enrolled first in school, they are often the first to be withdrawn in situations of economic adversity where local employment practices preclude the use of girl-child labour to generate cash incomes away from the home.

Whatever the national variations, it is clear that income growth and poverty reduction per se do not provide an automatic route to improved gender equity. The initial response within poor households to any increase in income may be to increase male enrolments, thus causing the gender gap to widen.

The case of Yemen graphically demonstrates the complex interaction between the gender gap and other disparities. Gender gaps in enrolment are exceptionally wide, with girls accounting for only one-third of children in Grade 1. However, the national average conceals large urban –rural differences, with girls far better represented in major urban areas.

In Sana 'a City, they account for more than 40 per cent of enrolments, compared with less than 20 per cent in rural Sana 'a. This is consistent with the broader pattern in many countries. In contrast to many countries, however, the correlation between wealth and the education status of women appears to be weaker in Yemen.

Illiteracy rates for poor and non-poor women are almost equivalent, at slightly above 80 per cent. Simply raising household incomes under these circumstances will have a limited effect, a fact that indicates the importance of more deeply rooted cultural factors.

Uneven progress in providing access to education has resulted in deep regional disparities within countries –disparities which, in some cases, rival those between rich and poor countries. Educational disadvantage tends to be concentrated in regions with the highest levels of poverty, as the following examples demonstrate.

Brazil. While Brazil is a middle-income country, the nine States of the northeast are among the poorest regions in the world. The poorest 50 per cent of the population in these States have per capita incomes broadly in line with the average for South Asia.This is the highest concentration of poverty in Latin America, with human-welfare indicators which are far worse than in the rest of the country.

Inequalities in education perpetuate the human-welfare gap between the northeast and more prosperous regions. Over half the children in the rural northeast receive less than four years of schooling, and one quarter of the population has had no schooling. The Philippines.The Philippines has achieved relatively high rates of net enrolment.

Regional differences related to poverty and service-provision account for much of this deficit. Four out of five pupils in Central Luzon complete primary school, compared with an average of one in three children in Northern Mindanao. Poverty incidence in Northern Mindanao is twice as high as in Central Luzon.

Over the past two decades, Indonesia 's progress in education has been impressive. Gender differentials have narrowed at all levels, and near-universal primary-school enrolment has been achieved. But issues of quality and progression through the secondary-school system have come to the fore, especially in the Outer Islands. Net enrolment rates vary between 100 per cent in Jakarta and 58 per cent in Irian Jaya; dropout rates are less than 5 per cent in Central Java, but 23 per cent in East Timor. The incidence of poverty on the Outer Islands is about 33 per cent, compared with 20 per cent in Java. Similar differences are observed in human-development indicators.

Some of the developing world 's widest educational disparities exist between Indian States. In Kerala, almost all children in the 10 –14 age group are literate. By contrast, one-third of boys and two-thirds of girls in Uttar Pradesh are illiterate. The difference can be traced back to the primary-school system. Around one-quarter of all boys and half of girls in Uttar Pradesh have never enrolled.

In the States of Bihar, Rajasthan, and Uttar Pradesh, the gender gap in enrolment is 25 per cent or more; in Kerala and Tamil Nadu it is less than 7 per cent. Inter-State differences have a profound bearing on the wealth gap in education, as noted above, there is a large national gap in enrolment between rich and poor households in India. But the wealth gap varies widely across States. In Kerala the enrolment gap between the richest 20 per cent and poorest 40 per cent of households amounts to 9 per cent; in Uttar Pradesh it rises to 56 per cent. This gap extends into children 's school careers. Attendance rates at school for children from the wealthiest 20 per cent of households are broadly similar for Kerala and Uttar Pradesh.

However, the attendance rate of children from the poorest 40 per cent of households in Uttar Pradesh is 48 per cent – around half of the rate achieved in Kerala. Such differences starkly illustrate the fact that poverty is not an automatic barrier to higher levels of educational attainment.

Public-policy choices, made in this case by State government, are capable of overcoming the disadvantages associated with low incomes. For instance, average incomes in Kerala are lower than in either Tamil Nadu or Punjab, yet nine out of ten children in Kerala complete Grade 5, compared with fewer than five out of ten in the two wealthier States.

Inter-State differences also have an important bearing on gender-related wealth gaps. The gender gap in enrolment for children from the poorest 40 per cent of households is close to zero in Kerala, but reaches as high as 32 per cent for Uttar Pradesh and 44 per cent for Rajasthan. As with other disparities, regional inequalities interact with gender disparities and urban –rural differences.

In Pakistan, the proportion of the overall adult population who have completed school to primary level or beyond varies from 26 per cent in Baluchistan to 41 per cent in Sindh. However, for rural women in these two provinces, the figures fall to 6 per cent and 8 per cent respectively.

Regional inequality on this scale draws attention to the need for public action to close the gap in opportunities for households in different parts of the same country.

Inequalities relating to ethnic minorities and indigenous people are strongly linked to regional disparities, and to the distribution of poverty. Deprivation in this area is among the most intensive of all forms of educational deprivation. But here too averages can have the effect of obscuring crosscutting patterns of deprivation. Within indigenous communities, inequalities based on household wealth and gender are often as pronounced as the inequalities in opportunity that separate indigenous and non-indigenous people.

East Asia has achieved some of the most impressive gains in education, increasing coverage and completion, and narrowing gender gaps. Pockets of intense deprivation associated with ethnicity remain intact, however. The case of the Philippines, which has achieved near-universal enrolment in primary school, illustrates the problem. During 1997, Oxfam conducted an education research programme in the Arakan Valley, in the eastern part of Mindanao island. The valley 's highland regions have been recognised by the government as the ancestral lands of the Manobos people. While the Manobos value education for their children, not least because they learn skills that are useful in negotiating with traders, schools are usually inaccessible. In one settlement covered by the Oxfam research project in 1997, the nearest school was a four-hour walk away over rough and steep trails. As a result, more than two-thirds of children were not in school.

The Philippines case is not untypical. Countries such as China and Vietnam are often held up as model performers, because of their success in achieving levels of educational attainment that compare favourably with those for countries at far higher levels of average income. In one sense, this is justified. But despite the rapid progress achieved in extending educational opportunity, ethnic minorities have often been left behind. Enrolment and completion rates in the 25 provinces with the largest ethnic-minority population are far below the national average.

In Vietnam, ethnic-minority groups living in remote, mountainous, and poorer areas –such as the Northern Uplands and Central Highlands –have far lower rates of enrolment and completion than wealthier regions such as the southeast. Although ethnic-minority groups account for only 13 per cent of the population, they represent half of the children who are not in school; and children of ethnic minorities make up less than 4 per cent of the school population. School-completion rates are also far lower for ethnic minorities.

Nationally, just over two out of every three students complete primary education. In Vietnam 's Central Highlands, the completion rate is 56 per cent. Research by Oxfam among Hmung communities in Lao Cai province in the Northern Upland region found enrolment rates as low as 40 per cent, and completion rates of only 38 per cent. Differences in educational opportunities partly account for the high concentration of poverty in the Northern Upland and Central Highland regions.

India 's caste system provides another stark example of education discrimination. Members of the 1091 scheduled castes and 573 scheduled tribes have historically suffered intense educational disadvantage. Often isolated both physically and geographically, these groups have lower enrolment rates, higher dropout rates, and wider gender gaps. Past discrimination is reflected in the fact that the literacy rate for scheduled castes and tribes is more than 30 per cent lower than the national average. Although there is evidence of disparities narrowing, this is happening at a slow pace.

Research carried out by Oxfam in the Indian State of Gujarat shows the persistence of inequalities related to scheduled tribes. More significantly, four out of every five children had dropped out of school by Grade 5, even though the overall completion rate for Gujarat is 50 per cent. In Latin America, indigenous people living in remote highland areas have simultaneously suffered simultaneously from exclusion and inclusion. They have more limited access to public education systems, and these systems often represent a hostile environment in which children are taught in an alien language in an institution that does not respect their culture.

In Peru, educational opportunities are concentrated in the coastal areas, with chronic under-provision in regions such as the southern highlands. By the age of ten, a child in Ayacucho, a predominantly indigenous area, will have received three years of education –one year less than a child in the capital Lima. Thereafter the disadvantages become cumulative, as the low quality of education takes its toll. Only one-quarter of children in Ayacucho complete primary school. On average, taking into account repetition and dropout rates, it takes 15 school years per child to finish primary education in Ayacucho, compared with seven years in Lima.

As in other regions, and with other dimensions of inequality, educational deprivation serves to reinforce poverty, with the most deprived communities experiencing the most severe exclusion.

In Mexico, the 'poverty belt 'states of the Pacific South account for more than 80 per cent of the incidence of subsistence poverty. Some 5 million people are affected, more than the number of extreme poor in all of urban Mexico. An estimated two-thirds of those who live in the municipalities with the highest degree of poverty are indigenous people.

Most of these municipalities lack access to basic amenities such as safe water and electricity –and they have the most limited access to education.

Illiteracy rates for indigenous peoples are five times the national average, and net enrolment rates 20 per cent lower. In municipalities with a proportion of indigenous people greater than 30 per cent, each adult has on average four years 'less education than the national average.

The strong association between education deprivation and poverty among indigenous people intersects with gender disparities. Indigenous people suffer extreme disadvantages, but indigenous women are particularly affected.

Indigenous people in Guatemala receive on average 1.3 years of schooling, compared with a national average of 4.2 years. Indigenous females receive on average half as many years of schooling as indigenous males.

In Bolivia, more than half of indigenous males and two-thirds of indigenous females do not complete primary education.

In Peru, one half of indigenous women have received only an incomplete primary education, compared with one-quarter of non-indigenous women. Education differences contribute directly to the high levels of income poverty found among indigenous people.

In Mexico, average monthly incomes in non-indigenous municipalities are twice as high as in indigenous municipalities. Human-resource endowments, as well as physical-resource endowments, contribute to the gap.

In Guatemala, there is direct evidence of the importance of education to income poverty. While indigenous people earn less than non-indigenous people with similar levels of education, those with the least education have the lowest incomes. Indigenous people with between 0 and 6 years of education receive less than half the average income of indigenous people who have 7 –11 years of education.

Bibliography

Auter, P. I., Hanna, M. S., 1996, "The Challenge of Developing Online Courses", *Paper presented at the Annual Meeting of the Speech Communication Association*, San Diego, CA, November 23-26, 1996.

Barbara K. Kaye and Norman J. Medoff, *The World Wide Web; A Mass Communication Perspective Mountain View,* Calif.: Mayfield Publishing, 1999.

Berge Z. L., 1999, "Interaction in Post-secondary Web-based Learning", *Educational Technology*, 39(1), pp. 5-11.

Birkerts, S., *The Gutenberg Elegies: The fate of reading in an electronic age*, Boston: Faber and Faber, 1994.

Bichelmeyer, B. A., Kiggins, E.A., 1998, "Using Web-based Conferencing in Post-secondary Instruction", *Proceedings of the Annual Conference on Distance Teaching and Learning*, Madison, WI, August 5-7, 1998.

Dieberger, A., *Supporting social navigation on the World Wide Web*, International Journal of Human-Computer Studies, 46, 805-825, 1997.

Forsyth, I., 1998, *Teaching and Learning Materials and the Internet* (2nd ed.), London: Kogan Page.

Ho, M. S., 1996, *Learning and Teaching in Cyberspace: An Empirical Investigation of Computer-assisted Instruction for Geography*, Academic exercise, Dept. of Geography, Faculty of Arts and Social Sciences, National University of Singapore.

Jones S., 1995, 'Understanding Community in the Information Age' Cybersociety; Computer-Mediated Communication and Community, S.G. Jones (ed) Thousand Oaks CA.: Sage.

Maddox, C. C., 1997, *The World Wide Web and School Culture: Are they Compatible?*, in D. L. Johnson, C. D. Maddux, and L. Lieu, (eds.), *Using Technology in the Classroom*, New York: The Haworth Press.

McAleese, C. Green, et al., (eds.), *Hypertext: State of the art*, Oxford: Intellect. 1997.

Michael J. Miller, "The Net Changes Everything", *PC Magazine* 18, no. 3 (9 February 1999.

Nielsen, J., *Hypertext and Multimedia: The Internet and Beyond*, New York: Academic Press, 1995.

Rheingold, H., The Virtual Community: Homesteading on the Electronic Frontier, *Reading*, MA: Addison-Wesley Publishing, 1993.

Tapscott, D., 1998, *Growing up Digital: The Rise of the Net Generation*. New York: McGraw-Hill Book Company.

Index